Peacemaking for Churches

The author is a lifelong Anglican and church sideswoman, a former PCC and
Sunday School teacher, Woodbrooke College or and
magistrate. She has been works for
ecumenical and inter-fai ions include
God is Looking After Me, ~~Elder Abuse and Mediation,~~ *Changes and Challenges in
Later Life,* and *Advocacy, Counselling and Mediation in Casework.*

BY THE SAME AUTHOR

God is Looking After Me (Church Information Office, 1968)

Elder Abuse and Mediation (Avebury, 1997)

Change and Challenges in Later Life (ed) (Third Age Press, 1997)

Advocacy, Counselling and Mediation in Casework (ed) (Jessica Kingsley Publishers, 1998)

Peacemaking for Churches

A Bible-Based Pastoral and Practical Guide

Yvonne Craig

First published in Great Britain 1999

Society for Promoting Christian Knowledge
Holy Trinity Church, Marylebone Road, London NW1 4DU

Bible quotations are from *The New Revised Standard Version of the Bible* © 1989.
The publisher and author are grateful to the following for granting permission to
reproduce copyright material:
Robert Willis, 'Let Us Light a Candle'. Reproduced by permission of The Very
Reverend Robert Willis.
Alan Gaunt, 'We Pray for Peace'. © Stainer & Bell Ltd, 1991.
Fred Kaan, 'Put Peace into Each Other's Hands'. Reprinted by permission of
Oxford University Press.
Rosamund Herklots (1905–87), 'Forgive our sins as we forgive'. Reprinted by
permission of Oxford University Press.
William Turton, 'Oh thou, who at thy Eucharist didst pray'. Reproduced by
permission of Hymns Ancient and Modern.

British Library Cataloguing-in-Publication Data
A catalogue record for this book is available from the British Library

ISBN 0-281-05177-1

Typeset by Wilmaset Ltd, Birkenhead, Wirral
Printed in Great Britain by The Cromwell Press, Trowbridge, Wiltshire

Contents

CONTENTS

PART THREE: Peacemaking for Christians and churches:
Ways forward

Acknowledgements

I wish to express my thanks to Richard Chartres, Bishop of London, for contributing a Foreword to this book.

I am also grateful to the many ministers from whom I have learned much about mediation in church and community conflicts, including

Canon Derek Russell, first Director, Whitstable Mediation
Revd Stanley Baxter, North of England Healing Trust
Revd John Blinston, former Secretary, Mediation UK
Revd A. Duce, Lincoln Prison
Revd Prof Duncan Forrester, Centre for Theology & Public Issues, Edinburgh University
Revd J. Foster, Chantilly, France
Revd Peter Knapper, Chair, Southwark Mediation
Revds Nelson and Ron Kraybill, Mennonite Bridgebuilders

My appreciation is due to countless members of the laity, especially clergy wives, Thelma Fisher, awarded an OBE for her work as Director of National Family Mediation, and Lisa Parkinson, another pioneer in conciliation.

Gratitude should also be shown to all my associates working in multicultural mediation, including Tom Daffern, Director of the Multi-faith and Multicultural Mediation Service, Peggy Cavello, Masana de Souza, Patricia Gonzales, Jesvir Kaur-Mahil and Manzoor Khan.

Lastly my thanks are due to Simon Kingston of SPCK who has encouraged and enabled this book to be published, and to Dr Philip Hillyer and Mary Matthews for their editorial assistance. However, I am responsible for any mistakes in it, and for its views unless credited to others. The book is dedicated to peacemakers everywhere known and unknown, and to those who need their help.

Yvonne Joan Craig

Foreword

The philosopher A. N. Whitehead observed that a 'deliberate aim at Peace very easily passes into anaesthesia'. For this reason it is essential for Christian people to abjure generalized hyper-moralizing about peace and instead to apply themselves with rigour to the biblical foundation of the rich tradition of Christian reflection on peace-building.

I am particularly grateful for the insights of this book since I am currently working with a Christian partnership to create a Centre for Preventing and Transforming Conflict in the City of London. We are rebuilding the Church of St Ethelburga, Bishopsgate, which was itself a victim of a terrorist bomb, in obedience to the example and command of the Prince of Peace. It is good that Yvonne Craig has pointed us to the wisdom of the scriptures and to the present possibilities of a practical translation of the hope they convey.

I commend this work to you. St Seraphim of Sarov once said that a single person with peace in their heart could convert the countryside for miles around. Yvonne Craig is concerned to help us grow into that reality.

+Richard Londin

The Right Revd Richard Chartres
Bishop of London

Introduction

Mediation: A ministry of reconciliation

Now I appeal to you, brothers and sisters, by the name of our Lord Jesus Christ, that all of you be in agreement and that there be no divisions among you, but that you be united in the same mind and the same purpose. For it has been reported to me by Chloe's people that there are quarrels among you, my brothers and sisters. *(1 Corinthians 1.10–11)*

We are all born to be peacemakers. This is because we are made in the image of God. *(2 Corinthians 5.18)*

We may be parents, printers or priests but we can all be peacemakers between people. In our families, workplaces and churches we can reconcile those who are divided by disputes. We can build bridges between people who are hurt by separation. Through compassion and love we can help to heal the wounds of those who suffer from differences, discrimination and despair.

We all have unique and special gifts for peacemaking, each in our own ways. Some are called to extra prayer. Others are called to action. Many have vocations in pastoral care, social work, advocacy, counselling and other helping activities.

This book readily recognizes the many varied paths to peacemaking for Christians and churches, but is written to focus on the way of *mediation*. This is mainly because Jesus is our model as a mediator, although he also came to fulfil many other roles, about which many other books have been written. His coming also led to conflict, although he worked for reconciliation.

Thus the aim of this book is to provide a biblical base and practical guidance about mediation for peacemaking in and for churches. It is concerned to decrease, not increase, the workload of over-stressed ministers, by providing resources to help fulfil their ministries.

It has three parts.

Part One has five chapters telling stories of the ways in which conflict has been coped with constructively in the Old and New Testaments, and in different contemporary situations. Part Two provides a practical guide to the potentials of mediation for churches. Three chapters, in turn, list the mediation principles, processes and skills of peacemaking, providing examples and cautions about good practice. Part Three has a conclusion discussing practical ways forward for developing Christian peacemaking, followed by an appendix pointing to the formal church codes which regulate congregational relationships.

This introduction shows the book's biblical basis, and its focus on Jesus the mediator, healer and peacemaker, yet who suffered from conflicts. The meanings of mediation, conciliation, counselling and advocacy are explored and the main principles of mediation are discussed.

It begins by linking the opening biblical text of a past story with that of a present one.

Trouble in a team ministry

Adrian was a lay minister and also a lecturer in religious education at the local college, so he seemed to be a good choice for leadership in a church newly planted by a team ministry. Soon he had started a Bible study group, which grew steadily in strength and numbers. So did his personal popularity, especially among young people.

Consequently, on the team leader's return from a month's mission to Africa, some lifelong church members complained that the congregation was becoming bitterly divided over Adrian's modern and not traditional teaching, as well as his authoritative academic style.

However, the team leader had good mediating skills. He brought everyone together to share in finding ways of resolving the conflict, saying that he did not want to impose his solution against their wishes.

It was eventually agreed that the young people would have their own Bible group, led by Adrian, whilst the team leader would take another, studying the same texts from traditional viewpoints. Every three months, both groups would meet together to share their experiences. It worked well!

This was the kind of problem that Paul was asked to deal with when Apollos, an Alexandrian Jew, who as a keen Christian convert and eloquent speaker, had been acclaimed as their leader by some local church members.

So nothing is ever new. Paul skilfully conciliated the conflict between those who said they followed Apollos, Peter, or himself. He reminded people that Christ, whom they should follow, could not be split among groups. Similarly today, ministers mediate comparable conflicts in their churches.

The sad schisms which separated the early Christians were condemned by Paul, as scandals ruined the reputations of churches. Today scandals are magnified unmercifully by the media, when many could be prevented by mediation.

So perhaps peacemaking for churches now is even more important than it was for the early Christians. We need to seek internal unity as the Body of Christ in our struggle against external evils. We are also called to make a contribution to peacemaking in the wider world with its bitter conflicts arising from injustice, war and painful poverty.

The biblical bases of mediation

'Jesus the mediator of a new covenant' (Hebrews 12.24) is the recurring subject of the letter to the Hebrews. In telling the Galatians that Christ was a mediator, Paul reminded them that 'a mediator involves more than one party' (Galatians 3.20). As he explained to Timothy, not only was Jesus the son of God, he was also a mediator between his Father and his human family:

> For
> there is one God;
> there is also one mediator
> between God and humankind,
> Christ Jesus, himself human,
> who gave himself a ransom for all
> *(1 Timothy 2.5–6)*

The death of Christ, described here as a ransom, is also called a new covenant in the Epistles and Gospels. Covenant means contract or agreement, and God made many earlier agreements reconciling the conflicts of his children, including those with Abraham, Noah, David and others, before Jesus came as the perfect peacemaker:

> For he is our peace; in his flesh he has made both groups into one and
> has broken down the dividing wall, that is, the hostility between us.
>
> *(Ephesians 2.14)*

Jesus is the model mediator for all those who seek to be peacemakers,
with the promise of blessings (Matthew 5.9) in the ministry of reconciliation which has been entrusted to us (2 Corinthians 5.19).

Although Jesus is our model of mediation for peacemaking in Christian relationships, the increasing use of mediation in the secular world
can be seen to follow the pattern of what Bishop John Taylor calls *The
Go-Between God*, in his book of that name:

> The third party makes the introduction, acts as a go-between, makes the
> two aware of each other and sets up a current of communication
> between them, and activates them from inside. *(Taylor, 1972)*

Here Bishop Taylor refers to the work of the Holy Spirit, but it is certainly also the recognized role of mediators who work in international
diplomacy, marriage mediation, commercial and community conciliation services and the many other forms of conflict resolution. All of
these refer to peacemaking, and the healing of personal and social relationships.

Mediation and healing

Mediation, in the *Concise Oxford Dictionary*, is defined as being a 'con-
necting link ... for the purpose of reconciliation', and is associated
there with the Late Latin word, *mediare*. Reconciliation, as a form of
social healing, has a double link with Jesus the mediator, as the Old
English word for him was *healend*, the one who heals and saves. Mediation heals the wounds between people, whereas the law can tear them
apart. How many ministers' marriages and careers have been destroyed
because conflicts over alleged or actual pastoral misbehaviour have
been taken to court, rather than settled privately and confidentially
by mediation?

However, mediation complements the law in that both are concerned
about justice and upholding human rights. Some lawyers refer relationship conflicts to mediators, and often also take mediation training themselves. In other cases, as when crime of violence threatens people, or
when legal entitlements are disputed, mediators will refer people to
lawyers.

Also, just as law can fail to heal conflict, so also may mediation, although research shows that the vast majority of cases are improved. This book is not uncritical of mediation, and its first part has a chapter about failures. It realizes that our contemporary world is complex, as are the regulations and organizations of modern churches. Mediation services should network with relevant authorities, to complement and not displace their work.

If this book appears simplistic, it is because it tries to follow biblical precepts of being simple, as was Jesus in his command about loving, and in his teaching through parables. This openness to the ways in which these have been interpreted and adapted to current contexts, inspires the beliefs offered in the book and respects its readers' discernment and abilities in learning to use mediation appropriately.

Counselling, comforting, conciliation and advocacy

We have already seen above that mediation is the work of the Holy Spirit. John, in Chapters 14 to 16 of his Gospel, also described this as that of Counsellor, Comforter, Advocate and Helper, according to the translation of the Greek *paraklētos*.

Whereas past wisdom thought that knowledge and experience was enriched by giving multiple meanings to words, today we analyse and attach them separately. Although comforting, helping and protecting are terms which apply equally to parents, professionals and the general population, counselling, conciliation and advocacy are considered by many people to be distinct processes practised by specialists.

This book does distinguish between the processes, but views them as working together in a mutually supportive partnership: co-operating not competing.

Counselling is viewed as therapeutic help given to individuals with inner personal problems. Advocacy (legal or citizen-based) represents the interests of those who feel unable to speak up for themselves. Conciliation (or mediation) is an *interpersonal* process, and brings people in conflict together to empower them impartially in reconciling their relationships and situations.

So, for example, clergy (especially priest confessors) and laity trained in counselling skills will help someone with an alcohol problem. Others, skilled in advocacy, will support disabled people in their rights of access to buildings. However, when there are conflicts in and among congregations, between churches, or with the community, mediation is very helpful. Mediators can be ministers or members of the laity.

Often ministers will need to use all these skills and processes, either with different people, or with the same person. An example of this would be a hospital chaplain caring for AIDS patients. He or she counsels them as they prepare for death; mediates between them, their partners and parents in conflicts about last wishes, and advocates on behalf of the sufferers in obtaining needed social services.

However the laity can offer a most valuable ministry in mediation, and significantly, most mediators are lay, although increasingly ministers are seeking training in skills which they rightly believe will help them safeguard the integrity of their churches and congregations.

Thus this book affirms the natural ability of most people to be peacemakers, and provides the basis for learning skills for useful voluntary mediation service in churches and elsewhere. It also acknowledges that increasing numbers of career mediators offer highly professionalized consultancy and assistance which may be needed in very complex international, commercial or ecclesiastical conflicts.

Here it is helpful to remind ourselves that ecclesiastical conflicts contributed to the rise of the early and current conciliar movements, concerned with medieval and modern disputes about increasing democracy in church decision-making. The word 'conciliation', like conciliar, has Latin roots, and is concerned with helping resolve conflicts by 'a voluntary settlement' (*Concise Oxford English Dictionary*). This is based on the democratic principle that people should have the opportunity to contribute to decision-making about matters which affect their interests and concerns.

Principles of peacemaking in church conflicts

The first among many principles is that of *acknowledging* conflict constructively as an opportunity for personal, interpersonal and congregational growth. Conflict is a normal and natural human process which is often necessary for personal and social change. It is how we deal with conflict which can determine destructive or positive effects. The Chinese symbol for crisis shows that as an occasion for dealing creatively with the conflicts of life.

However, too often, we tend to sweep under the church carpet all the human grubby grumblings coming from what the Old Testament calls being a 'slanderer among your people' (Leviticus 19.16). The

New Testament describes gossips as 'mere busybodies' (2 Thessalonians 3.11). Just as dirt gathers, so does gossip generate what Paul goes on to call 'envy, dissension, slander, base suspicions...' (1 Timothy 6.4). James calls this 'a world of iniquity' (James 3.6).

This can escalate into serious conflict in congregations, and disagreements and divisions. Untold and often unknown damage can be done because suppressed conflict can lead to personal depression and church apathy. Members may change churches and take their troubles with them. This widens worries and dissension.

Christians can be encouraged to confront conflict early. Then they can make choices about being empowered and enabled to deal with it compassionately and effectively.

The second principle is that of *affirming* respect for personal privacy and integrity through confidentiality. This extends normal pastoral responsibility for creating a church atmosphere in which members are assured that their personal talks with ministers or church officers are protected as private.

Balancing confidentiality with concern to confront church conflicts can be difficult, which is why we need to learn the relevant skills. Then the most competent and appropriate approach can be made to whatever kind of conflict arises.

The third major principle is that of *accepting* diversity. This means respecting the different hopes, fears and feelings that people have, and their various views and values. It is the anti-social behaviour which may result from conflicting ideas and opinions that can cause the most bitter disputes. Mediation is mainly concerned with encouraging people to change such behaviour, rather than argue about their inmost beliefs.

For instance, this book does not discuss ideological differences about abortion, disestablishment, 'high' or 'low' church practices, homosexuality, infant baptism, or women priests (to cite but a few in alphabetical order). However, it is concerned that people learn to express themselves about these issues in ways that are neither personally and socially hurtful and harmful, nor legally discriminatory.

From this perspective, philosophical or theological discussions about such issues are also to be accepted as opportunities to listen for the leading of the Holy Spirit, as well as to each other, as members of the Body of Christ. It is following comparable challenges, conflicts and changes throughout Christian history that the church has grown and developed into the worldwide ecumenical Body of Christ that it is today.

This acknowledgement, affirmation and acceptance of God's call to us to change, as persons and as congregations, needs to be balanced by our beliefs in the value of authority and traditions, and our awareness of the power structures within churches which affect relations between ministers and laity.

Here is another principle of mediation. It exercises no power over people through its gentle, non-coercive conciliatory processes. It can also provide an important Christian model in reconciling relationships of people in conflict. Mediation is essentially a process of bridge-building.

Bridge-building

Bridge-building is becoming an increasingly important contemporary Christian concept. Bridge-building between people is recognized as a mediation process in all forms of international and national diplomacy, as a prelude to, and as part of, peacemaking.

It is an activity in which we are all asked to participate, according to our abilities, in relations with our families, neighbours, work places, associations and churches. We cannot just leave this essential task to ministers, diplomats and professionals. Churches can benefit from having dedicated small teams of trained mediation volunteers who can be called on in crises and conflicts.

These peacemakers or bridge-builders, as such groups have some-times named themselves, can also offer their services to the outside community, as well as being available for use by their own congrega-tions, churches in the area and local ecumenical organizations. Media-tion may thus become a greatly valued part of the Christian mission to bring peace to the world. Churches could play a central role in this because their 'one foundation is Jesus Christ her Lord':

> Though with a scornful wonder
> Men see her sore opprest,
> By schisms rent asunder,
> By heresies distrest,
> Yet saints their watch are keeping,
> Their cry goes up, 'How long?'
> And soon the night of weeping
> Shall be the morn of song.
>
> *(Samuel Stone, 1839–1900)*

PART ONE

Partners in peacemaking: Ancient and modern

Blessed are the peacemakers, for they will be called children of God.

(Matthew 5.9)

So when you are offering your gift at the altar, if you remember that your brother or sister has something against you, leave your gift there before the altar and go; first be reconciled to your brother or sister, and then come and offer your gift. Come to terms quickly with your accuser while you are on the way to court with him, or your accuser may hand you over to the judge, and the judge to the guard, and you will be thrown into prison. Truly I tell you, you will never get out until you have paid the last penny.

(Matthew 5.23–26)

All this is from God, who reconciled us to himself through Christ, and has given us the ministry of reconciliation; that is, in Christ God was reconciling the world to himself, not counting their trespasses against them, and entrusting the message of reconciliation to us. *(2 Corinthians 5.18–19)*

1 Covenants and conciliation

Peacemaking in the Old Testament

It is not enemies who taunt me –
  I could bear that;
it is not adversaries who deal
    insolently with me –
  I could hide from them.
But it is you, my equal,
  my companion, my familiar friend,
with whom I kept pleasant company;
                    (Psalm 55.12–14)

David was one among many of the biblical characters who had painful conflicts with those who betrayed them. Promises of peace could not be trusted, yet he and they mostly met their challenges constructively in ways that led to positive change.

This chapter considers the Old Testament reliance on reconciliation and restitution in dealing with conflict, and God's covenanting or making agreements with his people through a combination of justice and mercy. Three stories of contemporary conflict resolution and reconciliation link our present experiences with those of the past.

Nevertheless the Old Testament is also full of the failures and follies of humanity:

My companion laid hands on a friend
  and violated a covenant with me
with speech smoother than butter,
  but with a heart set on war;
with words that were softer than oil,
  but in fact were drawn swords.
                    (Psalm 55.20–21)

3

Although David tried to reassure Saul of his loyalty, no reconciliation resulted. However Genesis 33 shows how Jacob did achieve reconciliation with his brother, Esau, despite the earlier deception and deprivation of his birthright initiated by their mother, Rachel.

The ancient story is an excellent example of good modern conciliation skills in conflict resolution. Jacob cleverly realized that he needed Esau's forgiveness and co-operation to make his proposed pastoral journeying possible. So humble apologies and gifts of reparation were offered and gratefully accepted by the warm-hearted brother. After deeply emotional embraces of reconciliation, the wounds of past family conflict were healed. Then the brothers began the practical problem-solving rather than blaming approach of negotiating their future plans.

The Old Testament is full of stories of conflicts and crises, beginning with those started by the serpent with Adam and Eve (Genesis 3). Then there was the cruel death of Abel (Genesis 4). Continuing conflicts marked Hebrew history right up to the destructive feuds between Jeroboam and Rehoboam which contributed to the collapse of Israel (1 Kings 11—12).

In another early story of strife between Abraham, Lot and their herdsmen, Abraham said to his nephew, 'let there be no strife between you and me' (Genesis 13.8) and they reached a reconciling agreement involving the division of land. So wisdom often prevailed in seeking resolution of conflicts.

Righteousness, reconciliation and restitution

Family solidarity and righteousness were regarded as being even more important in those times than it is now. Hence laws of restitution were central to all the regulations of Exodus 22, Leviticus, Numbers and Deuteronomy. These included detailed principles on which negotiation of different kinds of conflict should be based.

As far as violent crime, as distinct from conflict, was concerned, even the misunderstood penalty of 'eye for eye' (Exodus 21.24) was meant to *limit* the extent of more extensive primitive punishment.

The Ten Commandments (Exodus 20.1–17) referred to righteousness, or what recently has been called relational justice. Even though these only negatively ordered that neighbours were not to be oppressed, there was also a positive command, 'you shall love your neighbour as yourself' (Leviticus 19.18). Jesus developed this as one

4

of the two central commandments of his own ministry of love (Mark 12.29–31).

Early scriptural stress on the value of righteousness, reconciliation and restitution for peacemaking has been developed in the biblical theology of restorative justice based on God's many covenants with Israel and his continuing creation.

Covenanting then and now

A Christian dictionary definition of a covenant is close to that of a conciliation or mediation agreement. It is described as a bond entered into voluntarily by two parties, by which each pledges to do something for the other. Mediation involves a covenant depending on voluntary promises to restore relations through peacemaking.

We know how God made covenants with Abraham, Isaac, Jacob, Noah, and David, to name but a famous few. One of the essential elements of the divine contracts was that God would forgive Israel for its sins if the people would repent and rebuild relationships. Today this might be called rehabilitation.

It has specific relevance to the rehabilitation of offenders by probation officers who work with Victim Support groups and Probation Service Mediation and Reparation Projects. The following story shows this.

Racism and reconciliation

A teenager was caught scrawling abusive graffiti on a synagogue door. The magistrates said that this was a serious racist offence, but that as the boy had no previous criminal record, they would ask for a probation report. The probation officer found out that the boy was unemployed and homeless, having been abused at a children's home. The Rabbi was asked what he would feel about the teenager repairing the damage done, as he had no money to pay for a fine or compensation.

Both the Rabbi and the boy agreed to a mediation, at which the Rabbi gave a moving explanation of the way in which the graffiti had opened up the tragic wounds of the Holocaust racist persecution. The boy genuinely repented of what he had done, deeply apologized and promised never to do anything like it again, asking for forgiveness.

The Rabbi said he wanted to add to the importance of the mediation by making a solemn covenant in the synagogue, with both holding the Bible in their hands. This would include the boy's promise to clean and repaint the door, and the Rabbi's forgiveness on behalf of his congregation, together with an invitation to the teenager to be present at a short purification and rededication ceremony.

The probation officer reported the successful mediation and reparation agreement to the magistrates. They decided to discharge the young offender from court with a warning, and with a Binding Over to Keep the Peace.

In this example, justice and mercy were shown to be indivisible, as the Psalms, prophets and Proverbs proclaimed them to be: 'justice, and only justice, you shall pursue' (Deuteronomy 16.20).

Justice and mercy in peacemaking

Despite David's political experience, his psalms 'sing of loyalty and justice' (Psalm 101.1). Even though Hosea had a painful personal experience with an unfaithful wife, he still had the trust to say: 'return to your God, hold fast to love and justice, and wait continually for your God' (Hosea 12.6).

A beautiful illustration of justice and mercy in peacemaking comes in the famous story of Solomon. He mediated the conflict between two prostitutes who quarrelled about who was the mother of a little boy (1 Kings 3.16–28). Solomon carefully listened to the women's stories. He tested them with a question of practical problem-solving involving the child's possible death. This led to the true mother being identified and reunited with her child.

There are, of course, many examples in the Old Testament of situations when justice and mercy appear to be brutally divided, as in the cases of what might now be called ethnic cleansing when the Hebrews occupied Canaan. However it is not the purpose of this book to venture into biblical criticism and other debates, but to keep to its main aims.

Nor can this book describe Israel's systems of lawgiving, except to say that civil and criminal law proceeded from, and was integrated into sacred law. This was God's law, as the judges, kings and people perceived it to be.

People went for local justice to the city gates, where appointed elders would arbitrate or mediate their cases in informal but customary ways. Serious cases or appeals would go before Hebrew or other rulers. The ancient Hebrew processes of firm but informal justice and mercy were much more like the community and family mediation services of present society, than the Roman legal system with which our own law courts have historic links.

In general, justice and mercy are too often fractured today, as in international conflicts where mediators try to reconcile and rebuild relationships. However, two recent brief stories show the continuing concern for the unity of justice and mercy, in the interests of peace.

The Rabbi and the 'Troubles'

In Northern Ireland, a small Jewish community felt that it might have an important mediating role in the bitter conflicts between local Protestants and Roman Catholics. The Rabbi thought that the feuding Christians could accept his impartiality as a mediator because he did not share their faith or history. Yet he felt that they would trust him because they knew that he and his family had also suffered from religious persecution, torture and deaths, under Nazi oppression.

The Rabbi received his small congregation's permission to invite the local Christians and the police to a meeting in his synagogue hall so that they could negotiate arrangements for public safety during the next march. Not only did he mediate that meeting successfully, but thereafter, he and his community gave their hall for further discussions of local peacemaking in planning future marches. On each occasion, he introduced and closed meetings with invocations and thanksgiving to God for his justice and mercy, and prayers that the people of their island would learn to become peacemakers.

Betty and the Beth Din

Betty was a Jewish woman who had suffered from violent conflict with her husband. She wanted a divorce. She could certainly get a civil divorce, but she belonged to an Orthodox synagogue and knew that she should go to the Jewish religious court, or Beth Din. She would have to apply for a *git* to release her from her marriage vows. Otherwise her congregation would criticize her.

Despite the sympathetic hearing that was given to Betty at the Beth Din, with constructive suggestions that she should seek therapy from Jewish counsellors, the *git* was refused. Betty then learned that there was a Jewish family conciliation service, and also a Jewish Arbitration and Mediation Service. This had distinguished Jewish lawyers and other professional people who acted as volunteer mediators.

Betty went to mediation, having persuaded her husband to accompany her. He was now distressed at the thought of losing his wife, and possibly the custody of their children. To cut a long story short, he confessed his drink problem, which had started the angry conflicts and his aggressive abuse to his wife. He also promised to seek help from Alcoholics Anonymous, if his wife would agree to stay with him.

The co-mediators, a man and woman, helped the couple to draft a trial agreement about continued co-habitation, fixing a date for them to return in three months, or earlier, if conflicts continued.

As a general principle of mediation is to refer victims to the law or police for protection, should *active violence* occur, Betty and her husband were advised to take such action, should their agreement break down seriously. In fact, the marriage mediation was so successful that the couple later went on a second honeymoon!

In both these cases, of interest to Christians as much as to Jews, the process of mediation led to peacemaking in which justice and mercy were practically combined in a contemporary context. These stories show how we rely today mainly on trained volunteers to work in formal mediation services. In returning to this chapter's focus on Old Testament practices, we can see how the Hebrews coped with conflict.

Moses the mediator

Jethro was very concerned about the stress suffered by his son-in-law, Moses. He was exhausted by mediating and judging the constant con-flicts that his people brought to him in their hazardous journey through the wilderness.

Jethro could see that the people also suffered, as they had to stand all day long waiting to bring their complaints and conflicts to Moses. Some of them had travelled from distant camps. So Jethro asked Moses:

> Why do you sit alone, while all the people stand around you from morning until evening? . . . You will surely wear yourself out, both you and these people with you. For the task is too heavy for you; you cannot do it alone. *(Exodus 18.14, 18)*

Jethro advised Moses to 'look for able men among all the people . . . let them bring every important case to you, but decide every minor case themselves . . .'. He added, 'then you will be able to endure, and all these people will go to their home in peace' (Exodus 18.21–23).

So Moses chose respected and able people to share the task of conflict resolution with him, and we know from Hebrew history how this additionally developed into the Mosaic system of laws, and the increasingly powerful role of judges.

Scriptural texts describe Moses' role as that of judgement, because it was important to condemn idol worship in the courts. However his main concern was peacemaking between people, not adversarial approaches. He needed to keep his people together in co-operative solidarity, during the troubled times of the journey through the wilderness. He was also concerned, as has been indicated earlier, to fulfil God's law in combining justice with mercy, in ways close to modern mediation's principles and practice.

In his day, Jesus often condemned Jewish religious leaders and their formal legal system. This was because it seldom led to the justice and peace which the great prophet Isaiah had envisioned for the coming reign of righteousness when 'the wolf shall live with the lamb' (Isaiah 11.6):

> Then justice will dwell in the wilderness,
>> and righteousness abide in the fruitful field.
> The effect of righteousness will be peace,
>> and the result of righteousness, quietness and trust forever.
>
> *(Isaiah 32.16–17)*

It is clear that, then as now, seeking justice and peace is a difficult and never-ending task.

The foregoing old and new stories described human struggles to cope with conflict constructively in ways that led to peace. In many respects, the early church faced even more critical conflicts and challenges in peacemaking, as the next chapter shows.

> Lord, cleanse the depths within our souls
> And bid resentment cease
> Then reconciled to God and man
> Our lives will spread your peace.
>
> *(Rosamond Herklots, 1905–87)*

2 Conflicts in the early church

Peacemaking in the New Testament

For he is our peace; in his flesh he has made both groups into one and has broken down the dividing wall, that is, the hostility between us ... So he came and proclaimed peace to you who were far off and peace to you who were near; for through him both of us have access in one Spirit to the Father.   *(Ephesians 2.14, 17–18)*

As we know, the early church's attempts to reconcile Jews and Gentiles were marred by constant conflict. The passage above continues with an especially modern meaning as Paul tries to encourage new members for the church: '... you are no longer strangers and aliens, but you are citizens with the saints and also members of the household of God' (Ephesians 2.19).

This chapter relates some of the early church conflicts about circumcision, cleanliness and the breaking of the bread to current situations. It also shows Paul facing up to his own inner conflicts as he shares with the other apostles their united task of dealing with dissension and disputes, while strengthening the churches.

The reality of conflict was never more crucial than in the coming of Christ. Perceived as being a provincial preacher, and probably illegitimate by birth, Christ's challenges to rabbinical and Roman power structures, as well as to personal repentance and righteousness, led to continual conflicts and to the cross.

Christ's warning that he came to bring division among people (Luke 12.49–53), one of his 'hard sayings', showed the reality with which he recognized that his ministry would be confrontational and costly.

Early Christians also suffered as they continued to uphold Christ's challenges in building their church communities. Besides opposition from the outside that could result in execution, the early Christians had to weather severe internal conflicts. Yet they and we have been immeasurably enriched by the way in which these conflicts were confronted and transformed into means of growth and grace. The conflict over circumcision was, in every sense, one of the most painful.

The conflict about circumcision

Acts 15 is an illuminating apostolic account of how the early Christians constructively confronted the conflict about circumcision, and how they provided for us all an excellent example of good communication and conciliation.

Despite the fact that initially Paul and Barnabas got into a fierce argument with them about this (Acts 15.2), the apostles debated with the Judean envoys and then decided to go to Jerusalem to consult with Peter, James, John and the other church leaders.

> When they came to Jerusalem, they were welcomed by the church and the apostles and elders ... But some believers who belonged to the sect of the Pharisees stood up and said, 'It is necessary for them to be circumcised ...'. The apostles and the elders met together to consider this matter ... *(Acts 15.4–6)*

The Jerusalem Bible translation, which called this event the controversy at Jerusalem, gives a picture of Peter wisely waiting (as do good mediators) until everyone had expressed their thoughts and feelings. He then reminded them that God 'has made no distinction between them and us' (Acts 15.9), referring to the Gentiles. 'The whole assembly kept silence' (Acts 15.12), and after a period of reflection, James made his contribution.

'Therefore I have reached the decision that we should not trouble those Gentiles who are turning to God' (Acts 15.19). Circumcision should not be required of them, but they should follow certain other requirements of Jewish law (Acts 15.20). Through James' leadership, and that of the other apostles, the Jerusalem church reached a consensus. They agreed to write a letter of assurance incorporating their decision to the church in Antioch, where its members were the first to be called Christians. It begins:

> Since we have heard that certain persons who have gone out from us ... have said things to disturb you and have unsettled your minds, we have decided unanimously to choose representatives and send them to you, along with our beloved Barnabas and Paul, who have risked their lives for the sake of our Lord Jesus Christ. *(Acts 15.24–26)*

This passage is memorably moving because it shows the loving concern which early church leaders and their members had for one another, especially when their new Christian converts became involved in conflicts. All of Acts shows the courage of the church in confronting the challenge of the conflict over circumcision and, despite the dispute, dealing with it by such effective conciliation that it did 'much to encourage and strengthen the believers' (Acts 15.32).

Nevertheless, like life experience, success can often be followed by failure. So Acts 15, which began with Paul and Barnabas co-operating, ends with the sad story of their separation, due to their quarrel about John Mark. 'The disagreement became so sharp that they parted company' (Acts 15.39).

Paul and his inner and external conflicts

Paul's self-awareness and honesty shine through his letters, as he shares his feelings, negative as well as positive, in them.

It is comforting to know that one of the greatest Christians had his weaknesses, like us. On one occasion he wrote, 'Therefore, to keep me from being too elated, a thorn was given me in the flesh' (2 Corinthians 12.7). This affliction – we do not know what it was – could have added to his feelings of being an outsider. He was certainly very conscious that he had started out as a persecutor of Christians. Other passages indicate his turmoil, as he humbly confessed the conflicts afflicting his body, mind and heart: 'I do not understand my own actions. For I do not do what I want, but I do the very thing I hate', he accused himself (Romans 7.15).

He admits that, after his conversion, it was three years before he went up to Jerusalem to pay his respects. He only saw James then, and merely stayed for 15 days. He first met Peter 14 years later, during his next visit to Jerusalem (Galatians 1.17–18, 2.1).

Although Paul points to the positive achievements of his ministry among the Gentiles, motivated by the mission he received from God, one negative, if unintended, result of not wanting to preach in the patches where others were working (Romans 15.20) was inadequate communication, and poor personal relations with the Jerusalem church elders. On one occasion this led to Paul admitting that when Peter came to Antioch, 'I opposed him to his face, because he stood self-condemned' (Galatians 2.11) for apparently shifting his views about circumcision and relations between Jewish and Gentile Christians.

Blaming is not conducive to conciliation so the apostles had to move on, prompted both by the unity of spirit that bound them together, and the practical needs for solidarity and mutual support in their campaign to heal the disputes about unclean food.

The conflict about Cornelius and cleanliness

It was Peter's vision, following the earlier one of Cornelius, which led to the early church crisis about whether Christians could eat the same food as the Gentiles. Jews considered this ritually unclean. The crisis was compounded because 'the circumcised believers who had come with Peter were astounded that the gift of the Holy Spirit had been poured out even on the Gentiles' (Acts 10.45). 'So when Peter went up to Jerusalem, the circumcised believers criticized him' (Acts 11.2).

However, once again, through the peacemaking ability of the apostles, the conflict was gradually resolved. As Paul wrote on another occasion:

> Let us not therefore not pass judgment on one another, but resolve
> instead never to put a stumbling block or hindrance in the way of
> another.   *(Romans 14.13)*

Through careful conciliation the apostles found a food formula which would satisfy Jewish Christians, yet not destroy the dietary customs of the Gentiles. More important, this enables them all to break bread together as church members.

Unfortunately, this was also linked with another conflict connected with the many which arose as the churches and their administration developed. There was a dispute about the distribution of funds to widows. A quarrel developed between the Greek-speaking and native Jews (Acts 6.1), as the former claimed their widows were neglected.

The apostles also dealt with this dispute in a constructive and practical problem-solving way, which led to seven wise deacons being appointed and blessed by the Holy Spirit.

However, some disputes could not be dealt with by compromise, since the apostles considered these deserved discipline, as when drunkenness became a scandal.

The dispute about drunks

Paul confronted the Corinthians with a challenge in his first letter to them. 'When you come together as a church, I hear that there are divisions among you' (1 Corinthians 11.18). He then went on to reprove those who abused what was meant to be the Lord's Supper, by greed and drunkenness.

Paul subsequently transformed his negative warnings into a very positive homily about the meaning of the eucharist. He went on to remind the Corinthians of the wonderful diversity of gifts which the Holy Spirit had given them all. He then continued a spiritual circle by returning to the question of conflict, where speech can be 'a noisy gong or a clanging cymbal' (1 Corinthians 13.1).

He ended with his memorably inspiring call to Christian love. 'Love is patient; love is kind; love is not envious or boastful or arrogant or rude. It does not insist on its own way; it is not irritable or resentful' (1 Corinthians 13.1, 4–5).

It was this transformation of conflict into a means of growth, which became a means of grace and sanctified, reconciled and redeemed so many of the relationship problems of the early church. It is this loving concern for fellow members of the body of Christ, and for its unity, which can heal divisions. This deals with disputes by compassion and conciliation. Three brief stories illustrate this, and connect with those related above.

Rushing to judgement

Vestiges of the militant crusading attitude of earlier times in church history can colour the attempts we make to impose our views on others, in ways which they feel to be cruel and unchristian. Here let us remind ourselves that the principles of mediation expounded later on in this book support the right of people to hold their own views and express them appropriately, subject to the limitation that this does not harm other people.

The early church conflicts about circumcision were particularly painful because of the sexual as well as ritual aspects involved in the different beliefs which people passionately held. Today there are similarly sensitive issues concerning these, as the following stories illustrate.

Michael, the curate, had married the church Sunday school teacher with whom he had an agreed virginal courtship for three years. He then found he was unable to consummate the marriage, despite extensive counselling and medical therapy. His wife, who longed for children, had their marriage annulled, and moved away from the parish.

Some of the parishioners began to form a group gossiping about Michael as they thought he must be a homosexual, and they were against that, and him. The rest of the parish loved Michael and were very sympathetic towards him, and what they recognized he must have suffered. The rector valued Michael as a person, and as a good evangelist, and had a compassionate consultation with him.

Michael said that his vocation was now towards celibacy, and that he wanted to stay in the parish, provided that his presence did not split the congregation. The rector then began confidential conciliation with the group who were crusading against homosexuality. Gradually they reached their own conclusion that, in the context of the Christian gospel of loving acceptance of one another, they should accept Michael and pray for his difficulties. They also agreed that it would be wrong for factions to spoil the unity of their church.

Only one member of the group decided to leave the church, and the rest disbanded and, more important, asked Michael for forgiveness, which he gladly gave.

Cleanliness and ungodliness

People's search for purity has a primitive but healthy base, although it can be personally and morally manipulated. For example, some people smoke heavily, yet complain about the hygiene of others. Others call AIDS patients ungodly, as happened in the next story.

Charles was a hospital out-patient who had been greatly influenced towards Christianity by the chaplain who was helping to prepare him for death. Charles began going to his local church, where he was identified as an AIDS sufferer by one of the congregation.

She refused to shake Charles' hand during the giving of the Peace, and began warning other members of the congregation not to do so. A large group made a deputation to their minister about this.

As a good mediator, he decided not to impose his own wishes on them, but to give them information to help them decide their responses to Charles, based on the truth rather than myths about AIDS.

He reminded them that not only had Princess Diana shaken hands with AIDS patients, but so did all the clergy who ministered to them. There was no possibility of infection. He also reminded them of the apostolic message about 'unclean' food, and that godliness was shown by the words which came out of people's mouths (Matthew 15.18–20).

There was a mediated discussion, but one to which Michael was not invited because he was too ill. As a result, all members of the congregation shook hands with him during the giving of the Peace, and he felt so warmly welcomed that he spent his last weeks attending church services.

Breaking the bread

Emma, the 80-year-old widowed mother of her only daughter who had married a Roman Catholic, went to live in their granny flat. Emma was a devout Anglican, and when she accompanied the couple and their children to Mass, she was deeply distressed when the priest suggested she should convert to Rome if she wished to receive the sacraments.

Emma's son-in-law was a eucharistic minister. So he went to see the priest privately and said that he understood there was a discretion by which baptized people of other churches who shared Catholic views about the sacrament could receive it in a Roman church. Could the priest use this discretion, or would he prefer the family to consult the Bishop?

Unsurprisingly the priest agreed to pray about the matter. Shortly after, he called on Emma and said she would be welcome to come to the altar with her family, and receive Holy Communion with them. Unfortunately such an exceptional invitation might not now be given, in view of more recent Vatican rulings.

This concluding example of a conciliatory end to what could have been a disastrous dispute between family and church over the eucharistic love-feast, shows us, like the other stories, that now, as in the times of the early church, Christians can become involved in, but can also resolve, congregational conflicts.

In most churches ministers, now as then, consciously or unconsciously, formally or informally, use mediation principles and practices for peacemaking. At the same time they are concerned that these support rather than suppress justice. The next chapter looks further at some typical cases of church conflict and its resolution.

Peace in our hearts, our evil thoughts assuaging;
Peace in thy church, where brothers are engaging;
Peace when the world its busy war is waging;
calm thy foes raging.   *(Philip Pusey, 1799–1855)*

3 Challenges for clergy and congregations today

Peacemaking within churches

Who is wise and understanding among you? Show by your good life that your works are done with gentleness born of wisdom. But if you have bitter envy and selfish ambition in your hearts, do not be boastful and false to the truth. Such wisdom does not come down from above ... For where there is envy and selfish ambition, there will also be disorder and wickedness of every kind.

(James 3.13–16)

James 'the Elder' wrote his letter with such deep pastoral concern that he asks another painful but related question. 'Those conflicts and disputes among you, where do they come from? Do they not come from your cravings that are at war within you?' (James 4.1–2). He goes on to tell them that they 'covet something and cannot obtain it; so you engage in disputes and conflicts'. Later he tells them not to be 'double-minded' (James 4.8), and not to judge people behind their backs.

This chapter focuses on gossip, prejudice and discrimination, illustrated by recent stories. These follow, pointing to the firm teaching given by the apostles about seeking reconciliation rather than making church relations worse.

Paul and James preached a united message about the destructive effects of 'murmuring and arguing' (Philippians 2.14), and gossip. Paul warned the Galatians: 'If, however, you bite and devour one another, take care that you are not consumed by one another' (Galatians 5.15). James was more explicit:

And the tongue is a fire. The tongue is placed among our members as a world of iniquity; it stains the whole body ... a restless evil, full of deadly poison.

(James 3.6, 8)

Gossip and grace

Although gossip has been one of the stereotypes projected onto women, it is significant that the early Christian leaders addressed their cautions mainly to men, although Paul warns Timothy about young widows (1 Timothy 5.13). This was not just because they wrote in a male-orientated society. One of their main anxieties was that people were too often competing about status, rather than co-operating together for the community's spiritual benefit.

This competition remains at the root of much conflict in our church life today. Choirs can develop what Paul calls 'enmities, strife, jealousy, anger, quarrels, dissensions, factions, envy...' (Galatians 5.20–21) if certain singers appear unfairly to be favoured with the principal parts. Disharmony is the literal result, and members can leave both choir and church, to the loss of all concerned. It is trumpeted into the neighbourhood, where the local scoffers spread the gossip even further, and add malicious variations.

Organists and ministers can also become involved in longstanding and increasingly bitter conflicts about the choice of music for the church. They quarrel about what, when and how it is played, and for how long. Organists resign. The congregation splits into supportive and critical factions. The local newspaper headlines a vivid story about a parish plagued with management and musical mishaps.

Conflicts about status can become really counterproductive when enthusiastic members of church councils dispute over decision-making and leadership roles. Paul gave a solemn and salutary warning about not being 'puffed up in favour of one against another' (1 Corinthians 4.6). Major unresolved ecclesiastical conflicts catch the watchful eye of the press, and hurt local church reputations. These can escalate and cause suffering to the church at large.

Even more personally painful, perhaps, can be the gossip about the intimate relations of church people. There can be endless titterings about whether a Server is a celibate, sexually active, has HIV or AIDS, or is even just gay. Victims of such gossip have sometimes attempted suicide, out of desperation and depression.

There there is the gossip in women's groups, causing splits between Mothers' Union and Young Wives' members. Single parents and divorcees are too often scapegoated, or, through excessive good intentions, showered with gifts of Christian 'charity'.

Gossip about, and among, adolescents who are trying to shape their own lives, can drive them from church. Anxious young people can feel overburdened by advice, criticism and rules.

Perhaps the most severe problems develop when a church minister, warden, officer or elder becomes the centre of gossip, because of alleged impropriety with a member of the congregation, or another person. There can also be accusations of incompetence, neglect or even dishonesty in administering church affairs. Possibly alcoholism or other substance abuse is also suspected.

Ministers who have had pastoral training in counselling generally approach these situations on a confidential one-to-one basis to find out the truth. There may have been real wrong doing. If this is confessed, the damage done may be repaired. If a crime has been committed, recourse to the law, and/or church disciplinary codes may be necessary for all involved.

However, the problem may not be with others, but with ourselves. We all have a shadow side which can lead us into projecting our own weaknesses and failures on to others. Gossip can be based on wishing to seek attention for our emotional needs, whether these be for love, popularity or power. As Paul said, 'if those who are nothing think they are something, they deceive themselves' (Galatians 6.3). However, wise ministers now reframe this to assure insecure people that as everyone is important to God, it is wrong to degrade others.

Clergy, seeking to be peacemakers, also advise people to pray about problems, their own and the other individuals involved, so that they all grow in spiritual grace. This, of course, is necessary and valuable in all relationships, and may be the only possible course, together with confession and perhaps suggestions about therapy help. This is especially appropriate in very sensitive cases where people's inner conflicts are concerned.

However, there is a danger that prayer is recommended, sometimes unconsciously, just for practical purposes of suppressing conflicts between people. These can fester like unclean wounds that do not heal, when suppression causes deep depression, or serious repression.

Sweeping conflicts under the church carpet, rather than clearing them up, prevents courageously challenging them in a constructive way. Hiding conflicts prevents opportunities for repairing and rebuilding relationships in churches.

Reminding the early churches of God's grace, Paul exhorted Christians as follows:

> Do not be conformed to this world, but be transformed by the renewing of your minds, so that you may discern what is the will of God – what is good and acceptable and perfect.
>
> *(Romans 12.2)*

Mediation as well as meditation is a helpful way of 'renewing your minds' in changing attitudes to embittered relationships, as we shall see in the next story.

Meditation and mediation

Emma, a retired headmistress, had run the church prayer group in her home for many years, leading Bible readings and intercessions, followed by a quiet time for meditation.

Tom and Kitty, a cheerful and energetic young couple, had just joined the church after moving from the city, and attended services regularly with their two teenage children. They all started going to the prayer group.

Shortly after, Emma marched up to the Manse and told the minister that Tom was trying to take over her group, and that Kitty was filling the meditation slot with a babble of continuous prayer. The minister told Emma that they had come from a charismatic background, and reminded her of Paul's teaching about having respect for each other's diversities of gifts (1 Corinthians 12.4–11).

Emma left meekly, but a little later Tom and Kitty arrived saying that they had decided to start their own prayer group as the young people felt stifled by Emma's formality. The minister reminded them of Emma's long experience, and James' advice: 'let everyone be quick to listen, slow to speak, slow to anger' (James 1.19).

To cut a long story short, the second group formed, attracted away the young people from the first one, plus many others in the congregation. Soon it was divided down the aisle, with Emma's members on one side and Tom's on the other. What was worse, Emma and Tom were openly hostile to one another, in divided camps. Some members in distress drifted away from the church and the rest became increasingly miserable.

The minister, trained in mediation skills, knew that all those affected by conflict should have the opportunity to voice their views in contributing to decision-making about how to resolve it. So he called an open meeting for members, and asked everyone, in turn, to comment on the situation. In a not unsurprising consensus among Christians, everyone said that they wanted to do the will of God and what was best for their church.

The minister then encouraged them to discuss the issues that were causing such painful divisions, while assuring them that all sincere and selfless prayers to God, however different, were acceptable and good. He thus earned their trust because he spoke affirmatively, yet impartially.

The spiritual sharing together of the place that prayer had in their lives, developed deep mutual sympathies as well as learning among the members. They soon moved on to asking themselves how they were going to be able to make the most of all their diversities of gifts, in the unity of the Spirit, instead of dividing the church.

The minister than offered his Manse for the weekly prayer meetings. Emma suggested that she, Tom *and any other prayer leaders* could take it in turns to run evenings. Tom wondered if two or more rooms could be used so that the different groups could be active at the same time. All could join together for refreshments, and walk each other home.

Everyone felt that it would be good to take time in reflecting on the advantages and disadvantages of these and possible other options. So it was generally agreed to meet in a month's time to finalize arrangements with the minister's blessing.

The following Sunday the church was full. Emma, Tom and Kitty were sitting together and everyone else was happily jumbled up together. Their minister had shown them how much he valued each of his flock by listening to them. So they followed his example, and also, renewing their minds, soon found a generally acceptable plan for their future prayer groups.

> Do nothing from selfish ambition or conceit, but in humility regard others as better than yourselves. Let each of you look not to your own interests, but to the interests of others. Let the same mind be in you that was in Christ Jesus. *(Philippians 2.3–5)*

The baby and the dog

Two sad conflicts divided the Parochial Church Council. A young single mother, who had never been a church member but lived in the parish, had just had a miscarriage in hospital, although half of the PCC suspected it was a late abortion. She asked the rector if the baby could be buried in the churchyard, but there was some bitter opposition to this.

At the same time the local landowner, who was a benefactor of the parish, also asked for his wife's pet dog to be buried in the churchyard. Again, the PCC was angrily divided over this.

Even more disconcertingly, the disputes became increasingly fractioned.

Passionate arguing about the power of the gentry and the powerlessness of the poor became linked with generally latent party politics. One of the PCC threatened to write letters to the local and national press about what he believed could be disgraceful decisions of discrimination. Another PCC member suggested invoking the ecclesiastical legal authorities.

The rector, a well-known peacemaker with some knowledge of mediation principles, reminded the PCC of Paul's challenge to the divided Christians in Corinth. 'Can it be that there is no one among you wise enough to decide between one believer and another?' (1 Corinthians 6.5). The rector then asked every member of the PCC to ponder and pray privately about the issues of humanity which were involved, before he invited each to give a reconsidered review at the next week's meeting.

At this, tempers had cooled because the rector had previously wisely allowed people to ventilate their feelings completely. All PCC members gave their views calmly. Most agreed that, after reflection, they felt that it would be lacking in Christian compassion to deny a little resting place for the baby's body. There was a similar majority for allowing the dog's body to be buried in a spare small plot near the shed of the gardener, who had also loved the pet.

Even the two minority members congratulated the rector on consulting the PCC in such a fair and democratic way, especially as the decisions were ultimately his responsibility.

Pride, protocol and processions

Conflicts in churches today can involve their leaders, just as they did in the early church. Currently archbishops, bishops, the 'higher' and all the 'lower' clergy of the Church of England are still embroiled in acrimonious arguments about the ordination of women priests.

The introduction to this book has already made it clear that its aim is not to discuss differences of theological, philosophical, political, or any other opinions which people have the right to hold, but rather to consider the social acceptability of the behaviour with which they promote their views.

This chapter's concluding story, therefore, deals with a conflict among cathedral clergy concerning the duties of their new colleague, a woman priest. Although Martha was officially welcomed by all, and given scrupulous respect in all public references, she was excluded by some of their clergy from personal invitations to their private social gatherings.

The dean deplored this, but felt that he could not formally interfere with clergy family arrangements, although he knew that Martha had hurt feelings. However, the unpleasant situation reached a crisis, when the undercover conflict became manifest during planning for a visit by a female foreign Minister of State.

She had specifically asked for a woman priest to hostess her, and to preach the sermon at what was to be an important civic service of welcome. The Chapter meeting became a hive of discontent, and, as Martha felt, a nest of discrimination.

> A dispute also arose among them as to which one of them was to be regarded as the greatest. But he said to them, '... the greatest among you must become like the youngest, and the leader like one who serves'. *(Luke 22.24–26)*

This well-known rebuke of Jesus to his most trusted disciples as they argued about who should be the greatest among them certainly applied to that Chapter meeting. Pride, protocol and processional status were the dominant issues. Clergy who disapproved of women priests blamed their existence as the cause of the most serious cathedral conflict they had ever experienced.

The dean knew of his responsibility to direct the ordering arrangements, but he was wise enough to know that if the underlying conflicts were not confronted, the discontent would eventually erupt elsewhere. This could have possible publicly disastrous consequences in the cathedral and in the Anglican, ecumenical and national press. Yet he was concerned that his ultimate decision might be seen as partial. This could prejudice future relations with his clergy.

So he suggested that one of the archbishop's honorary staff, a retired bishop, universally respected for his fairmindedness, holiness, and humour, and for being a skilled mediator, should be asked to moderate an informal meeting of the Chapter on the subject. This idea was accepted by all.

The bishop invited people, in turn, to put forward their own preferred proposals for clergy participation in the civic service, but stressed that these must focus on practical issues, and that no platform would be given to proclamations about the ordination of women. The problem-solving not blaming principle of mediation would be paramount.

Having previously vented their irritation and frustration about their foreign guest's requirements which had been imposed on them, the clergy then calmly made varied suggestions. The bishop reflected back to them what he understood them to say, so that they recognized he had actively listened to their options.

He then asked them all to meditate for five minutes on Luke 9.46–48, Jesus' response to the disciples' dispute on preferment, which the bishop read to them, before seeking guidance on what might be called God's option.

After a long period of silence Martha spoke first. She said she would like to convey to the State Minister's staff, the pleasure and privilege she would have in hostessing their visitor at the reception afterwards, but that the Dean should have the customary honour of escorting her to the Cathedral service.

The most senior canon, a traditionalist, then spoke and said that Martha's sermons were excellent, and that he would like to propose she gave one on that occasion. There was general assent to these suggestions, and then the Chapter easily worked out the processional and other aspects of the service. Peace had been restored, and relationships improved.

> For all thy Church, O Lord we intercede;
> Make thou our sad divisions soon to cease;
> Draw us the nearer each to each, we plead,
> By drawing all to thee, O Prince of Peace;
> Thus may we all one bread, one body be,
> One through this sacrament of unity.
>
> *(William Turton, 1856–1938)*

4 Ecumenical conflicts

Peacemaking between churches

So if I come, I will call attention to what he is doing in spreading false charges against us. And not content with those charges, he refuses to welcome the friends, and even prevents those who want to do so and expels them from the church.   *(3 John 10–11)*

John's letter to Gaius, one of the early church leaders, supports his ministry, and rebukes another 'who likes to put himself first, does not acknowledge our authority' (3 John 9). It was this type of factional conflict which led to divisions among the first Christians. It continued throughout the following centuries to contribute to the disunity of separated churches.

People are still being excommunicated from some churches because they have merely attended others, or threatened with it because of intermarriage conflicts. This is the subject of one of the three stories which this chapter tells. Another deals with a dispute about alleged discrimination involving ministers from white and black churches. The first story describes welcome acts of reconciliation taking place in Belfast.

However, in reminding ourselves of John's warnings about negative divisions among churches, we know that there were many positive influences of reform, piety and leadings of the Holy Spirit. These enriched the formation of the different denominations as they exist now.

Also it is true to say that former denominational conflicts have largely been replaced by the welcome ecumenical movement of the present century. This is grounded on the well-loved prayer of Jesus: 'Holy Father, protect them in your name that you have given me, so that they may be one, as we are one' (John 17.11).

Yet attitudes of religious snobbery and dislike still exist. So the warning of James, 'do not speak evil against one another, brothers and sisters'

(James 4.11) should be remembered by all Christians. It applies especially to those caught up in bitter long traditions of hatred and anger, as in the religious and political warmaking of Northern Ireland.

A story of peacemaking in Northern Ireland

Libraries are filled with books about the religious and political conflicts of Northern Ireland, about which governmental attempts to find overall solutions are now being actively renewed with inter-church co-operation.

They are keenly supported by ecumenical groups such as the Corrymeela, Crossroads and other communities, social organizations such as the mediation network for Northern Ireland, and informal mixed Christian bodies such as the Peace People.

Our first story concerns one of the battle-line areas of Belfast, where nearby Protestant and Roman Catholic churches are like fortresses in their concern for the physical as well as emotional protection of their members. Families keep themselves separate, but sometimes children make friendships which overcome enmities.

Bridget and Kirsty met at the local library story-reading group. They found themselves laughing at the same jokes, began sitting together regularly, and discussed the idea of swopping their own books. Bridget invited Kirsty to her home, but then suddenly remembered family rules, and asked her if she was a Prot. Kirsty said that she was a Presbyterian but that her mum was a Peace Woman so it was OK for her to make friends with Catholics.

The children agreed to get their mums to 'phone each other, and it transpired that both their husbands were angry that their children each suffered from jeers when they went to their respective church services.

Kirsty's mum suggested that Mr Hussel, a teacher from the one mixed, non-denominational school in the area, who did voluntary work for a mediation service, could be invited to deal with the difficulties, as he was a Mennonite and independent of the main denominations involved.

By this time the children were enjoying not only each other, but also the prospect of standing up for their own wishes against their fathers' fears. They both nagged their parents into agreeing to a meeting of families at the school in question one evening.

Mr Hussel warmly welcomed them all, enabling everyone, children and adults, to describe fully their feelings about the situation. The parents, who had never spoken to 'the enemy' before, realized how nice and normal each family was, and shared mutual sympathies about the plight of their children suffering taunts.

The mediator then asked them if they could think of any remedies, and it was not long before Kirsty's father offered to call for Bridget and escort her past his own chapel until she reached her parish church. Bridget's dad then made a similar offer. Soon after, both mums invited the children into their homes for teas of soda bread and scones with lots of cream and jam. There was a real peacemaking party!

In case it should be thought that this simple story is an insignificant example of mediation, it should be stressed that inter-church mediators, invited by the police, have been continuously and critically involved in reconciliation activities. They have brokered important deals relating to arrangements for marches and public meetings, as well as in many very serious individual and group cases of conflict.

Conflicts are always more painful and problematic when groups as well as individuals are involved, as in the next story where racial as well as religious discrimination was alleged.

Binding the brethren

So then you are no longer strangers and aliens, but you are citizens with the saints and also members of the household of God ... In him the whole structure is joined together ... in whom you also are built together spiritually into a dwelling place for God. *(Ephesians 2.19, 21–22)*

Ezekiel, a Pentecostal church minister, belonged to a clergy consortium concerned with inner-city ministries. Despite all the Equal Opportunities proclamations of the ecumenical hierarchy, represented by the rural dean as chairman of the group, Ezekiel felt that Paul's encouragement to the Ephesians had been disregarded.

As a British West African, Ezekiel still felt he was regarded as a stranger and foreigner, even though he was born in England, and educated at Oxford University. He felt himself to be the perpetual outsider, always being passed over for promotion. Although his church was the fullest in the area, his white clergy colleagues never made him feel welcome among the 'members of the household of God'.

When the rural dean retired from the chair, it was informally passed on to the senior minister of the Anglican Evangelical church and then to the Methodist in charge of the local circuit, and Ezekiel felt angrier and angrier at not even being considered.

The Baptist minister, James, who had worked in an African intermediate development project, perceptively understood the problem. Ezekiel was antagonizing his colleagues by channelling his anger into continual protests about racial discrimination against *other* black people. They thought he had a chip on his shoulder, and continued their traditional policy of choosing chairpersons based on seniority.

James was a natural mediator, but decided that this was a situation which needed healing with quiet shuttle diplomacy. He approached Ezekiel confidentially, sympathizing with his feelings, but invited him to consider that it was seniority, not racism, which was the issue.

He added that this also affected the women clergy who had not been so long in the ministry, and who suspected sexism. Ezekiel remembered that some of his own black female congregants complained about domineering attitudes by their menfolk. He realized that he had to rethink his views on discrimination.

James then confidentially asked the current chairman to consider whether it would be progressive for him to recommend a more modern model of ecumenical partnership and sharing. This would be made visible if chairs were taken on a year's rotational basis. In this way each church would have a turn, and it would be clearly demonstrated that there was no wrongful racial, sexist or any other kind of prejudice.

James added that this would also be an important symbol and sign of their inner-city ecumenical co-operation, with a clear message for improving multicultural community relations.

This story ended well, with the ecumenical clergy group establishing a good local reputation for promoting policies against discrimination. Also the quiet unpublicized initiative of James was an example of how mediation principles support those of social justice.

Mediation is also an important process in establishing marital justice. Sometimes the rights of couples who love one another can become in conflict with those of their churches who have strong social doctrines about their members' religious duties, as our third story shows.

Marian, Malcolm and marriage

St Peter was a married man. So were some subsequent Popes, before the Roman Catholic church's commitment to celibacy for its clergy developed.

Early church leaders insisted on the importance and reality of the new life that filled people as they learned to know and love Jesus. They wanted it to overflow into their love for each other, and not cause conflicts.

> Rid yourselves, therefore, of all malice, and all guile, insincerity, envy and all slander. Like newborn infants, long for the pure, spiritual milk, so that by it you may grow into salvation. *(1 Peter 2.1–2)*

Today, if couples are keen members of different churches, then ecclesiastical questioning can painfully threaten pre-wedding discussions with clergy. Marian was blest, because her Roman Catholic religious obligations were presented by her priest in a negotiable way. Malcolm's Anglo-Catholic vicar trusted his faithful Server to avoid convenience conversion.

This chapter does not intend to go into the history, evolving theology and varied social developments concerning mixed marriages. It just follows one story which appears to be typical of the best mediated pre-nuptial arrangements.

A recent Papal Nuncio to Britain once remarked that every parish priest should be a mediator, and Fr Brian, who was Marian's confessor, was an excellent example. He consulted with Fr Ian, Malcolm's vicar, who had confidence to leave discussions in the hands of his Roman colleague, whom he knew to have fair-minded sensitivity about marital relationships.

Marian and Malcolm went to her church and Fr Brian began by congratulating them warmly, and then asking them both what *they* felt and thought about the connection between their future family life and their churches. The young couple had previously given this very careful consideration, and said that they had already decided to maintain their own separate loyalties in receiving the sacraments, but that each would alternate in accompanying the other to their Sunday services.

Fr Brian gave them a very positive affirmation of the wisdom of their decision, and then asked them how they wished to handle the religious education of their children. They said they would take their children with them to their shared services, and leave them free gradually to make up their own minds about which church they wanted to join formally at confirmation. However both promised to give the children full Catholic teaching, while pointing out different Anglican and Roman perspectives.

Fr Brian said he could understand this decision, although official rules were clear that Roman Catholic mothers should have their children baptized and brought up in their Faith. As a compromise, would the couple agree to Roman baptisms?

The couple brightly said that they thought that recent Anglican and

29

Roman theology was focusing on *adult* or late baptisms. Then people could knowledgeably make their own commitment. They were concerned that if the babies were baptized as Roman Catholics, they would later feel guilt if they decided to settle in their father's church, or vice versa. They both had the same firm feelings about this.

Fr Brian hummed a bit, but said that he respected their conscientious decisions, and that although it was not in the canons of either church, it might be possible for Fr Ian to arrange a simple non-liturgical family service of reception into his parish. However the Roman Catholic bishop would have to be consulted to see if Fr Brian could be given some dispensation to arrange a comparable service, in order to maintain Marian's family links with her own church.

The couple breathed a sign of relief, and Marian promised that she would faithfully continue her own religious duties of confession and attendance at Mass, while Malcolm, with a smile, asked Fr Brian if he could canonically agree to being a godparent without a baptism. He replied that they would have to see if ecumenical relationships evolved as far as that by the millennium!

In this story the priest did not have to mediate between a couple in conflict themselves, but his experience of the mediation approach enabled the young couple to make their future plans based on understanding and co-operation with their churches.

In too many other cases, clergy religious zeal and inter-church rivalries can drive hard doctrine into wedges between people, who stop coming to church completely.

This last story began with reference to Peter's concern for Christian marriage. Paul repeated this in his letter to the Ephesians, where he described all of our human relationships as having the potential to unite us into one body. This echoed the prayer for unity by Jesus in John's gospel. Paul, with his usual practical common sense, suggested how Christians should do this:

> I therefore ... beg you to lead a life worthy of the calling to which you
> have been called, with all humility and gentleness, with patience,
> bearing with one another in love, making every effort to maintain the
> unity of the Spirit in the bond of peace.   *(Ephesians 4.1–3)*

We can learn much by meditating on this text as we review our ecumenical relationships, and renew our commitment to peacemaking.

We pray for peace
But not the easy peace,
Built on complacency
And not the truth of God.
We pray for real peace,
The peace God's love alone can seal.

(Alan Gaunt, 1935–)

5 Findings and failures

Peacemaking and problems

We look for peace, but find no good; for a time of healing, but there is terror instead. We acknowledge our wickedness, O Lord ... for we have sinned against you.

(Jeremiah 14.19–20)

Our human weaknesses and sinfulness lead to many failures in our lives and relationships. We fail to love. We fail to forgive. We fail to make peace. Following the biblical teaching about love and forgiveness in peacemaking is central to mediation. Its principles, processes and practices reflect this. We also find that human failures in learning to grow internally, and to apply this teaching, restrict its progress.

We find that the different personalities that God gives us are sometimes shaped by the temperaments, attitudes and beliefs we develop into hardened moulds which fail to expand in co-operative social relationships. We find too often that people express their identity through maintaining anger, hatred and unresolved conflicts. We find that the peacemaking processes of mediation, like the words of the Bible, sometimes fail to touch the heart or speak to the spirit of those who try its services.

We also find that religious beliefs are used to cement people into fixed positions and enmities, instead of liberating the charity and compassion to which Christians are called. Thus it is said that no conflict can be more prolonged and painful than a church conflict. Everyone claims that God is on his or her side. Failures of human pride, and of being closed to the guidance of the Holy Spirit, can lead people to refuse mediation, or, indeed, counselling and other forms of personal and pastoral help.

Human failures also affect mediators and can spoil their work. Failures of insufficient knowledge, inadequate skills and insensitivity to spe-

32

cific human needs, especially in complex situations, can prolong rather than prevent conflict. Peacemaking is full of failures and problems.

Yet we also find that mediation failure may be short rather than long term. There may be a failure to make agreement about a present conflict, but the learning experience may prevent another from developing. So it is important that we are wise about the limitations of mediation, but not cynical in refusing to consider it. The following stories show some of its pitfalls, but also its potentialities for transforming failure. For failure not only needs to be faced, but also offered to the grace of God for transformation.

A conflict about a cult

Becky, aged 18, was the victim of a religious cult. Her experience illustrates those which can lead to severe breakdowns in personal, family and social relationships. These affect people in such deep emotional and spiritual ways, and may involve the police and legal protection of young people, so that mediation may be undertaken as a last resort, and often prove inappropriate.

However Christian ministers may feel, like Titus, that they have a duty to intervene in situations where 'There are also many rebellious people, idle talkers and deceivers ... they must be silenced, since they are upsetting whole families by teaching for sordid gain what it is not right to teach' (Titus 1.10–11).

Nevertheless, today some ideas, like those of mystic, creation and Celtic spirituality, and others within the Christian range of New Age thinking, encourage people to explore God's mysterious and wonderful ways of working in the world. These ideas, often ancient rather than new, often helpful rather than harmful, are especially attractive to young people searching for understanding in the modern world.

Thus it is important to have information and accurate knowledge in discerning cults from mainstream religion, and to be wise about using mediation when conflicts occur, as they did in Becky's family.

Becky's parents were very proud of their only daughter who had just got her first job. Becky was shy, but her self-confidence grew rapidly and her eyes became glazed. Mary, her mother, suspected that a little 'first love' was developing. John, her husband, started being anxious, quarrelling with his wife who told him not to play the heavy father.

This is where, too often, increasingly bitter and painful unresolved conflicts can develop between parents, leading to an oppressive misery-making atmosphere in the family home. This can drive young adults into resentful silence, or leaving home prematurely. Paul's advice is timely here. 'Fathers, do not provoke your children, or they may lose heart' (Colossians 3.21).

Mary and John were used to give-and-take discussions, despite their potentially explosive emotions, so they then sat down and calmly assessed the fact that Becky appeared to be naturally taking her first steps to independence. She needed their caring, but careful, support.

So they asked her if she would like to bring any new friends home to supper one Saturday, and were delighted the following week when David arrived with flowers. He was well-groomed and polite, and asked if Becky could visit his home the following week.

For the next month, the visits alternated, until David asked if Becky could stay the weekend with his parents to join in their family house worship.

These weekend visits continued, and Becky's eyes grew even more glazed. She shared with her parents the feelings of warmth and inspiration which filled her at the love-feasts of Father Samuel, David's parent. Mary and John became worried, and asked if they could visit the place.

Becky sensed her parents' growing hostility, packed her bags and left home, leaving a 'Don't worry ... see you soon' note. John and Mary immediately contacted their minister, Timothy, and asked him to act as a mediator between David's family and theirs, to bring Becky back.

Timothy told them that the self-styled Father Samuel had the reputation of attracting sexual services from his young female followers, with the assistance of his son, but that he would visit them and try to mediate.

When he called, he was politely told that Becky was 18 and free to choose her own way of life and companions. David's father, showing awareness of mediation, pointed out that Timothy was really just acting as an advocate for Becky's family, and that he was not an independent, impartial third party. Neither David's father, nor Becky, as she reached for his hand, would consent to mediation. She said she wanted to stay there.

Her parents took anti-cult advice, sent her leaflets, phoned and wrote to her, but to no avail.

However mediation was helpful later, as it can sometimes help to repair relationships after cults have been left in despair, which eventually happened when Becky found herself replaced by another girl. Becky went to see Timothy, who informally mediated between her and her parents about a return home. He helped them reach a no-blame agreement in which Becky accepted arrangements for counselling, and Mary and John said they would not pry into the past unless and until Becky felt able to confide in them.

Timothy asked if the family were ready to join with him in a prayer asking for forgiveness and renewed loving relationships, and then Becky, Mary and John hugged one another. Peace returned to their hearts and to their home.

A conflict with a charity

Tom, aged 40, had just become unemployed. He invested his redundancy money in a truck to help him start his own small transport business.

He then saw an advert from a local charity which was collecting food and clothing for poor families in Europe, and wanted it transported there. Tom and his family were interested in the idea of him working for a venture which publicized itself as a universalist religious body. He signed a year's contract.

For the next three months Tom had the time of his life, collecting bundles, which his wife helped him sort, and then driving them across the Continent to depots in small east European countries. He was paid reasonably, if not well, although he noticed that the charity organizer had moved into a smart office, installing computers and a young secretary.

Then a national newspaper's investigative journalism exposed a scandal in the countries concerned. Donated British goods were being syphoned off to middlemen who resold them elsewhere. Although his charity's depot was not named, Tom and his family were deeply shocked. They shared their anxieties with their pastor.

He offered to mediate with the charity's director to see if Tom's contract could be cancelled amicably. Tom was delighted but his boss was not. He refused to accept mediation, saying that Tom must finish his year's contract, otherwise civil action for breaking it would be taken. When the pastor asked if the boss had taken into consideration the recent exposure of wrongly administered charities, the answer threatened libel action.

At that time there was no firm evidence that Tom's firm was involved in any scandal, so no allegation about this could be supported, and used informally in mediation, or formally in court, to justify him refusing to finish his contract. The pastor did not have the detailed knowledge or experience with which to raise other issues which might have encouraged the director to agree to mediation. Nor did Tom have any savings to risk court action.

The pastor was distressed that mediation had failed, but Tom appreciated that it had been attempted, and both agreed to pray about the situation. It suddenly came to Tom, after meditating on the moral and legal challenges facing him, that his contract only provided for him to deliver goods to certain villages on agreed dates. It did not state names of the recipients, probably for bad, rather than good reasons.

So when Tom made the next delivery, he drove around the poverty-stricken outskirts of the village, and distributed the goods widely to its individual residents, avoiding the collection centre. On his return to Britain, his boss greeted him angrily, and said his services were no longer wanted. This, of course, was just what Tom wanted too.

A conflict involving discrimination and discernment

The next story shows the inadequacy of mediation on its own, unless supported by general cultural change. This is often the case where discrimination is involved. It is complicated by the fact that, at the time of writing, it is only in racial, rather than religious discrimination that legal action can be attempted in the UK. In this sad and sensitive area, the law also too often fails to bring redress.

The story merits a preface to explain why mediation was tried as a sign of its concern to fulfil biblical teaching about social justice. Readers of this book will not need to be reminded of the shameful history of Christian discrimination against Jewish people. The horrific Holocaust and Shoah stories still bring belated apologies from some official Christian bodies.

Christians also faced persecution in the past, as some black churches do today. Recently a black gospel choir had a National Front Nazi swastika sprayed on the door of their church in the East End of London. Ironically, it had once been a synagogue which also had had swastikas daubed on it.

Shared suffering can create common bonds, and many mediation services have volunteers who are Jewish, Christian, Muslim or come from diverse communities, working together in peacemaking.

> These are the things that you shall do: Speak the truth to one another, render in your gates judgments that are true and make for peace, do not devise evil in your hearts against one another, and love no false oath; for all these are things that I hate, says the Lord. *(Zechariah 8.16–17)*

The Hebrew word for peace, *Shalom*, is an ordinary daily greeting for Jewish people, while the sharing of the Peace has become an important part of church liturgies. The Psalms (29.11; 85.8; 125.5; 147.14), to number but a few, are close to the hearts of both Jewish and Christian peacemakers.

However, peacemaking in inter-faith relationships needs to be extended to citizens who have other religious beliefs. In Britain, Muslims form a large group who also suffer from discrimination. Yet Islam (which means 'enter into peace') shares the faith in one God. It pays respect to Jesus and Mary in its sacred texts. Its Kalimas, the five pillars of belief, prayer, fasting, almsgiving and pilgrimage, complement the Ten Commandments.

Unfortunately, it is the fundamentalist, extremist and bigoted aspects of Islam (like those of Judaism, Christianity and all religions) which are so alarming (especially in international peacemaking contexts, with which this book does not deal).

Many different kinds of religious or cultural conflict can develop in and between families, with neighbours and between diverse Faith groups. However, the gentle, respectful and co-operative process of mediation can provide a helpful process towards improving community relations, although in this next story it failed to resolve the bitter disagreements about cultural changes in a small village. This was mainly because mediators do not attack or try to change people's beliefs.

Fighting over inter-faith relations

Cross-cultural relations too often turn into *cross* cultural relations. This happened in an idyllic rural village when a British Asian company owner wanted to buy a crumbling old mansion. It had been derelict for 20 years. He wanted to restore it so it could house a Hindu Cultural Centre.

The local vicar, Simon, was immediately approached by his Parochial Church Council to see if he could mediate in the many conflicts which arose among the parishioners and villagers as they reacted to this news. The hope was that resolution of the conflicts would enable them to present a unified voice and agreed recommendations when the planning inspector came to hold a local environmental inquiry.

There were two main camps, which were very hostile to each other. In addition, many individuals had their own strong views, and those of the local landed gentry were dominant. There were fears about being swamped by robes, rituals and noisy coaches. There was even a sense of terror that their village would be taken over by foreigners. There were parental anxieties that their young daughters would be enticed into harems, and that their sons might be lured into weird meditation practices.

On the other side there were villagers who kept the few remaining local shops. They believed that the newcomers would help to keep the post office open, encourage the bus company to restore the much-missed transport services, and, of course, commercially benefit their fading trade.

Some individuals took extreme views about keeping heathen immigrants out of Britain. Others felt that they should welcome opportunities for mass missionary conversions. Many felt that they should just say 'no' to any change that was too difficult to think about.

Simon decided to call a public meeting in the church hall which he would chair. He called himself the moderator of the meeting, and intended to use his awareness of mediation principles to see that everyone had a chance to air their views fairly.

This story has to be shortened, and it will be no surprise to learn that, despite the best of Simon's intentions, the meeting turned into an uproar. Speakers would not stop talking. They interrupted each other. They became angry and insulting. They took no notice of Simon's efforts to control the disorder. They would not listen to each other, nor to Simon's repeated call for them to focus on each divisive issue in turn, and try to agree about constructive recommendations. Four hours after the meeting had commenced, many people still wrangled, as they did later on the way home, while others crept away exhausted.

The mediation was a failure and sad Simon felt a failure too. He went to his spiritual advisor who counselled him about coming to terms with his feelings over such a difficult situation. Simon was also advised to talk to the diocesan community relations officer, and to seek professional guidance from the co-ordinator of the city mediation service.

Both advised him to make an immediate round of personal pastoral visits to those who had been so angry or upset during the attempted mediation, in order to heal hurts and let them ventilate their views and feelings really fully. After actively listening, and showing that he had understood their present attitudes, he could then offer them corrective information about the proposed Hindu religious practices which might dispel prejudices and help them to develop practical options over issues to recommend at the planning inquiry. The aim would be to rebuild community peace.

It was also suggested to Simon that had he made these individual visits first, also explaining the way in which a mediated meeting has to be controlled fairly, the dominant voices would have already expressed their emotions, and subsequently been more able to participate reasonably in democratic decision-making and peacemaking.

He was also advised that a useful strategy in mediating large meetings is to ask people to form small groups discussing suggested topics (which might have been gathered from preceding pastoral visits). Their spokesmen (often local leaders) would be responsible for reporting back their group's recommendations on a specific issue to the large meeting for general acceptance.

Simon wished that he had known more about mediation processes, and he certainly found that by making the advised pastoral visits, hurts in the village were gradually healed, and people made their points at the inquiry in well-informed and temperate ways which gave a good Christian impression. Simon felt that their failures had been transformed.

There was also general relief when the Hindus' proposals were made known. They wished to build a private road over their land so that their members could travel direct from the major road, bypassing the village, and they would plant screening trees all round the estate, as well as restoring the outer facade of the house to its original Elizabethan style. They gave assurance that the centre was to be used for spiritual retreats and conferences, and that none of their music would be heard outside. Their planning application eventually succeeded.

Many of the villagers were disappointed at this, and even if the initial mediation had not failed, it would still have been unsuccessful in changing people's traditional views. So this story, unlike the others, did not have even a relatively 'happy ending'.

There are other cases when mediation fails to overcome difficulties, or where it is inappropriate as when there are legal disputes over church property, the employment of staff, and changes in prescribed religious services. However, even when the highest and cleverest church administrators and lawyers are called in, conflicts can still be unresolved, escalating painfully and publicly in the press.

This chapter has suggested some of the areas where caution and care has to be used if mediation is to be appropriate, realistic and effective. Each human relationship and situation is unique, and there are no fixed formulae which can be applied in considering how to approach conflicts. Christians, both church ministers and laity, need to seek God's guidance in prayer.

The next part of the book describes how the potentials of mediation can be practically realized by developing its principles, processes and skills.

> Love, all hatred has destroyed,
> Rendered all distinctions void:
> Colour, race and factions fall
> Thou, O Christ, art all in all.
>
> *(Charles Wesley, 1707–88)*

PART TWO

The potential of mediation skills and services

Those conflicts and disputes among you, where do they come from? ... Do not speak evil against one another, brothers and sisters. Whoever speaks evil against another or judges another, speaks evil against the law and judges the law; but if you judge the law, you are not a doer of the law but a judge. There is one lawgiver and judge who is able to save and to destroy. So who, then, are you to judge your neighbour?   *(James 4.1, 11–12)*

If another member of the church sins against you, go and point out the fault when the two of you are alone. If the member listens to you, you have regained that one. But if you are not listened to, take one or two others along with you, so that every word may be confirmed by the evidence of two or three witnesses. If the member refuses to listen to them, tell it to the church ...   *(Matthew 18.15–17)*

At that time I will change the speech of the peoples to a pure speech ... they shall do no wrong and utter no lies, nor shall a deceitful tongue be found in their mouths ... The Lord has taken away the judgments against you ... I will remove disaster from you ...   *(Zephaniah 3.9, 13, 15, 18)*

6 Principles of mediation

Peacemaking values

I ask not only on behalf of these, but also on behalf of those who will believe in me through their word, that they may all be one.   *(John 17.20–21)*

We are all called to be peacemakers. We are all given peacemaking abilities, alongside those which enable us to love and forgive. We can also be peacemakers in different ways, whether we are young or old, ministers or laity.

This third part of the book focuses on how we can contribute to the potentials of peacemaking through mediation, and this chapter deals with its principles.

However, like the following two chapters which offer practical and specific guidance about peacemaking processes and skills, it does not set out to provide an accredited training and qualification in mediation.

It cannot do this. Mediators, like counsellors, advocates, pastoral care workers and most social helpers, need to learn and practise in training groups, with the aid and supervision of those who have the necessary knowledge. Then practical experience of actual mediation is needed before we can call ourselves mediators.

Nevertheless we can all start immediately, or continue, to use our mediating abilities, and it is important to understand the ethics on which this should be based.

Ethics for mediators
The main principle is that we should try to reach a good standard, so that we really help rather than hinder people who are trying to resolve their conflicts. It is difficult to do this on our own. It is best to become a member of a mediation service, especially if it is run by local churches, Christian or community organizations. There we can have free ongoing training and evaluation. We can also pay for private professional courses.

Having said this, it is of course recognized that many clergy and church members from relevant backgrounds have been trained in communication skills, in negotiation procedures and in personal and public relations. They may also have a life-time's knowledge of helping people with their personal and social conflicts, so that they may have more practical experience of mediation than others.

Significantly, it is often those with most experience who are humble enough to know that they need to learn more. They generally prefer to do their healing work quietly in the background. For them, it is the work, not the label they wear, which is important.

There are no hard and fast rules in mediation, which is not a regulatory process like law, but only an ethical expectation that all those called to be peacemakers try to uphold its values and follow its major principles.

Some of these are now set forth in the form of brief notes in order to aid focus and discussion. The use of the alphabet, and repetition of key words, is meant to aid memory and quick recall, although this may irritate a few readers. It should also be stressed that the substance of these notes is in general use by other mediation trainers, although they may present them in their individual ways to fit specific mediation services.

The A, B, C and D of mediation principles

Acknowledging the need for peacemaking means
* that peacemaking must be based on justice, and not used to suppress or conceal conflict;

* recognizing that conflict can lead to positive change, and that, badly handled, it can be destructive;

* seeing the need for early, sensitive approaches to prevent disputes widening;

* accepting that mediation is only one of several ways of approaching conflict, and that it should be used appropriately;

* understanding that mediation is a voluntary alternative to legal action, which people retain the right to take, and that it is complementary to the courts;

* being aware that mediators share some but not all skills with advo-

cates, counsellors and other social helpers, and should respect roles and boundaries;

* confessing that we may be part of the conflict, and that then we need independent mediators.

Affirming personal identity and integrity in peacemaking means respecting

* the individual worth of people, and their human rights;

* their personal needs for privacy, and protecting their confidentiality;

* the natural abilities of those involved in conflict to confront it constructively, and empowering them in reconciliation and resolution;

* the responsibility of people to express their views in ways that do not offend or harm others, and ensuring socially acceptable behaviour;

* the duty of mediators to be impartial, non-judgemental, following mediation principles, and avoiding personal power-seeking.

Accepting diversity in peacemaking means recognizing

* that each individual is unique and developing, and that stereotyping and categorizing is wrong;

* cultural and social diversity, and learning to understand and respect different traditions;

* disability diversity, and the special needs of vulnerable people;

* gender diversity, and discounting personal prejudice;

* the diversity of human perceptions of truth, and respecting honestly held beliefs.

Bridge-building in peacemaking means bridge-building

* by bringing people in conflict together, and asking for their consent to mediation;

* between minority and majority groups and respecting equal opportunity principles;

* by considering all options for settlement, and exploring paths to peacemaking;

* by long-term commitment to reconciliation, and avoiding superficial solutions.

45

Communication in peacemaking means talking with people

* in culturally understandable ways, and without paternalism or condescension;

* on the basis of freely given consent, and without unwanted persuasion or pressure;

* with impartiality and by power-balancing, and not taking sides;

* truthfully and clearly, and exposing lies and misperceptions;

* courteously and fairly, and listening attentively and with empathy to all;

* about values, and reminding people about unacceptable, discriminating, offensive and violent language or behaviour.

Difficulties in peacemaking in churches occur because

* Christians may hold different deeply felt and long-established views, and either find it hard to express these without upsetting others, or prefer to prolong rivalries;

* congregations concerned about their reputation may fear that confronting conflict will exposure failures;

* clergy who know little about mediation may resent lay members seeking to start or support such peacemaking initiatives;

* church officers may be anxious about mediation destabilizing their power, or increasing not decreasing their burdens;

* lay people may prefer emotional dependence on being directed how to resolve conflicts by church leaders;

* churches often have hierarchical relations with different levels of accountability which can slow local progress;

* disputes over doctrine and social morality can seldom be resolved by practical agreement;

* poverty, poor housing and health, and unemployment are among the many structural difficulties which cause conflicts that require more extensive approaches;

* human failure and sinfulness prevents us from being willing to confess our faults and ask for forgiveness.

However, most of these difficulties can be overcome, or at least relationships and situations can be improved. This has been witnessed, not only by the early churches, but also now by Christians who practise mediation skills and use mediation processes.

It is the principled use of these mediation processes, informally and formally, at every stage of approaching church conflicts, which can bring clergy and congregations together in building and enriching their relationships. The next chapter describes these processes in detail.

> Let us light a candle in the darkness,
> In the face of death a sign of life;
> As a sign of hope where all seemed hopeless
> As a sign of peace in place of strife.
>
> *(Robert Willis, 1947–)*

7 Processes of mediation

Peacemaking ways

Put things in order, listen to my appeal, agree with one another, live in peace; and the God of love and peace will be with you. *(2 Corinthians 13.11)*

This chapter describes the basic process of mediation in simple steps, with memory aids, and illustrates this with a story about a quarrel involving an organist and choir member. It then describes the different forms that mediation can take, with brief examples suggesting which may be most appropriate for different kinds of conflict.

However, first it is important to introduce the ideas of co-mediation and the preliminaries to peacemaking.

Co-mediation

As the name implies, it means two mediators working together in resolving a conflict.

Co-mediation has many advantages. It is a good working model of two people co-operating together to resolve conflicts. It demonstrates their good communication with each other in sharing the problem-solving tasks. It enables mediators to be matched with those in conflict: a man with a man and a woman with a woman, young and old, and so forth. It provides ongoing opportunities for mediators to check with each other that they are following good practice.

However, it is realized that many ministers mediate on their own, either because they have to, or because they have already earned the trust and respect of their churches for impartiality and peacemaking. Also the laity, and Christians generally, may find themselves individually in a bridge-building or mediating role.

So this chapter addresses all peacemakers, recognizing that co-mediation is used most often when churches have set up trained teams.

Co-mediators can be helpful particularly in preventing people from suspecting that a single mediator favours one of them. They may reveal that they think that 'wrongful events took place behind closed doors' in the first stage of talking with each person separately and confidentially about the conflict.

Preliminaries to peacemaking

A good minister will generally be the first to observe that two church members are heading for a serious conflict, or one may make a confidential complaint. In the private interview, the minister will listen attentively and non-judgementally to the account given, then reflect back what has been heard. If it is appropriate, the minister will then ask whether the complainer will agree to a mediation. This is fully explained.

If agreement is freely given, the minister will privately approach the other person involved, stressing confidentiality and not reporting what the complainer has said. The minister will listen, reflect and explain as before. After consent, practical arrangements for the mediation meeting in some neutral venue are made.

These preliminary visits provide valuable insights into the causes and development of the conflict. They provide private space for people to share the relevant facts and feelings. They can help to ventilate the deep emotions which can cloud reason. They assure people that their pastor is taking their troubles seriously and sufficiently early to prevent them getting worse. Arrangements for meeting soon can limit this.

Of course, there are many instances when ministers receive complaints about which people are prepared to do nothing, or seek counselling for themselves alone. Obviously ministers have a wide range of pastoral services from which they can draw the right help to suit situations.

This chapter can consider only those situations where mediation is freely chosen by all involved as being the best bridge-building process available, and the next section suggests sequences of steps which have been found to be generally helpful, although linked by others in various ways.

It is stressed that these are not to be followed mechanically, as mediators have to use discernment, discretion, experience and intuition, in gently guiding people, in ways that most help them, through the stages of healing personal relationships and improving situations.

It is also stressed that the stages noted below may appear to over-simplify what is generally a profound and positive experience for all involved. Mediations often take about two hours, as they include all the courtesies of making people comfortable, giving them intervals for drinks or private reflection, and respecting their personal needs.

In addition it is suggested that in Christian (or other religious) mediations, it is good to start the meeting with prayer invoking the guidance of the Holy Spirit, and end it with thanksgiving. This is generally when there is resulting reconciliation. Even if it is only partial, or if a further mediation has to be planned, it is important to thank God for blessing increased mutual understanding. This in itself can start later and longer processes of healing between people.

Thus mediation seldom fails in bridge-building, even though peace cannot be immediately manufactured.

In this chapter's illustrative story the minister, Mark, learned that Barry, the new young organist, wanted to get rid of Arthur, the 86-year-old choir member. His solos were now faulty. Arthur was bitterly resentful and stirred up supporters, but both men hoped mediation would bring peace before the coming choir tour.

M E D I A T E at the meeting:

M   Make introductions
E   Exchange accounts: listening and reflecting
D   Discuss issues in conflict
I   Indicate options for settling conflict
A   Assist people in problem-solving
T   Test negotiated proposals' practicality
E   Encourage agreement and reconciliation

M: Make introductions

Mark introduced briefly the seven stages of the mediation, reminding Barry and Arthur of the relevant principles. Each was invited in turn to give an account of the trouble, without being interrupted by the other. Mark said he would then reflect back to each what he had heard to check misunderstandings.

E: Exchange accounts

Arthur began as he was the complainant. He described his anger and distress, after 40 years in the choir, at young Barry's criticism and tactics in trying to get rid of him. Mark reflected back the *feelings* and *facts* of Arthur's pain and long service.

Barry then said his music college education helped him to raise the standard of the choir so it could tour and fundraise for the church. Plans would be spoilt because Arthur's solos were slow to enter and follow the tempo. Barry wanted a younger choir member. Mark similarly fed back Barry's feelings of frustration, and the facts about the tour for church funds, and need for a new younger choir member. Both men said Mark had got it right.

D: Discuss issues
Mark then asked both men to list the conflict issues, so that each could be discussed in turn. The first was Arthur's replacement by a young man. The second was his singing. The third was Barry's unkind behaviour to Arthur. The fourth was Arthur's grumbling to the choir.

I: Indicate options
Mark asked the men what ideas they had for dealing with each issue. Arthur suggested finding a new choir man anyway, and said he would give up singing solos if he could still stay in the choir. Barry said he hadn't realized till then how deeply distressed Arthur was, and said he was sorry for being rude. Arthur admitted he was disloyal in grumbling and would stop.

A: Assist problem-solving
Mark congratulated the men on their progress and asked them to discuss any problems about the ideas. Barry said the tour coach only took 20, but Arthur said he could follow in his own car. Barry said that Arthur couldn't manage some modern music, but Arthur promised only to sing whatever Barry directed. Both men were prepared to apologize to each other.

T: Test negotiations
Mark asked them how in practice they would repair the damage to choir morale caused by the conflict. Both men agreed that, at the next rehearsal, Barry should make a short statement. He would say that after discussing tour plans with Arthur, he decided that he no longer wished to sing solo, and hoped that a new choir member would take his place. Barry would also say that he was grateful to have the valuable experience of Arthur staying in the choir.

E: Encourage agreement

Mark said that it would be useful for them both to have their own simply written agreement listing the four issues resolved, which they and he would sign, but which would be private and confidential. He then congratulated them again on having resolved their conflict, and reaching reconciliation.

Review and evaluation

Mediators review and evaluate their work, and Mark noted that he had resisted giving both men ministerial advice, the hallmark of clerical professions. This enabled them to work out the conflict themselves. It was an empowering experience in personal growth for them. It was also a learning lesson in communication and conflict management which would help them in future life troubles.

Mark had moderated the mediation carefully by stopping the men if they interrupted each other. He had pointed out that when people do this, it stops them listening and showing respect.

He regretted that he had forgotten to introduce and close the meeting by saying how much he and the church valued both men for themselves, as well as for their services. This mutual affirmation of esteem (or just of personal respect) inspires trust and confidence in the mediator. It is important in creating a warm and encouraging atmosphere for peacemaking.

This incident was of *face-to-face* mediation, which is always the first choice for peacemaking between people. Sometimes it is not possible. Thus this chapter continues with considering other types of mediation, to which the same principles and guides apply.

Shuttle mediation

Shuttle mediation is often called shuttle diplomacy, as it is generally used in the early stages of international peacemaking. The mediator acts as a go-between, carrying messages between people in conflict. They are guided from negative to positive stages of negotiation and agreement.

This was what happened in the story of the celibate priest. It may be the only way of bridge-building between people in very sensitive situations. Others may not want to meet each other for various reasons. In some serious domestic conflicts partners may be living separately.

It can also be useful in conflicts between churches, different denominations, faiths and cultures, where initial ground-breaking work has to be done in building foundations for mutual understanding.

In all cases, however, mediation aims at eventual face-to-face meetings between the main people involved to ratify any agreements reached, although sometimes this is only achieved in correspondence.

Shuttle mediation relies on the exceptional skills of convincing people to trust the fairness and impartiality of the process. They need assurance that the only messages carried will accurately repeat what people wish said, and not include anything confidential.

The mediator is ethically bound not to substitute personal preferences or judgements, although it is difficult to exclude interpretations and misperceptions, which continually need re-checking.

Telephone mediation

This is a variety of shuttle mediation, and is often used when there is trouble between people who live at a distance, such as estranged relatives and friends facing a crisis.

It can also be useful between clergy in a circuit or diocese where problems erupt from time to time and peacemaking is required. Busy church leaders and directors of religious organizations may not have the time to meet to deal as urgently as is required with an emerging conflict.

Also ministers and lay members who have a growing reputation for being good mediators may be asked for help on the 'phone by people they do not know.

But telephone mediation is limited if it does not eventually lead to some personal healing encounter. Yet it can usefully start the process of bridge-building, and introduce people to the principles which can be followed.

Correspondence mediation

Correspondence mediation may, perhaps, be the form which is most known to clergy in their pastoral ministry. Also people in general often try to sort out their disputes by writing letters in the first instance, especially to neighbours with whom they never talk.

The potential and limitations of this method are similar to those of telephone mediation. They are less positive because human speaking and involvement is avoided. This may be for weak reasons, but sometimes for good ones. We need to accept that a few people can only experience peace if they are left alone – and leave others alone.

Group mediation

Group mediation, or small and large group facilitation as it is often called, is especially valuable for churches where congregations should be consulted about important collective issues. It is also helpful when church or Christian groups face making difficult decisions.

Even though clergy and church officers may have the ultimate responsibility for finalizing decisions, congregations will accept these more happily when they feel that their contributions have been made, discussed and considered.

Mediation principles and processes are perfect for church decision-making. These can minimize clergy authoritarianism. They can maximize the laity's feelings that they are valued members of an open and democratic body. Respect is given to each person's contribution to discussions. No-one is able to dominate these if the meeting is moderated well by a minister, church officer, or nominated independent person who has mediation skills.

Churches who use group mediation generally advertise the issues of meetings well in advance and offer opportunities for prior private personal consultations, written suggestions and visits to the housebound. Everyone has time to clarify and exchange ideas.

Ideally, people are welcomed to an attractive setting where they can first enjoy a simple common meal, that bonds them together. The meeting opens with a blessing, and people are invited to sit in a circle. Platforms, which unduly exalt people, and large tables which create the atmosphere of courts and judgement, are to be avoided.

Without repeating the principles and processes already listed which are adapted to small and large group meetings, it may be helpful to add one or two amongst many other available ideas.

The moderator can ask the meeting to consent to a framework where one person does not speak twice or more, until all have had their turn in speaking once.

People are also asked to set their own time limits to the meeting, agree to an agenda and abide by the courtesies of not interrupting others, or using language which may be offensive to them.

A flip chart should be used to record people's suggestions (omitting their names), and then re-grouped into issues. If these, and the members, are numerous, the moderator can ask if the meeting would favour splitting up into small groups, each working on specific issues (with large papers and pens). They then report back to the re-assembled large meeting, which will discuss recommendations. All the paperwork will be displayed on walls for people to see their work.

Although this will be familiar to most people who attend workshops, at least one aspect may be different. In a mediated meeting, the moderator makes no moves or ordering without first asking the assembly's agreement to procedures.

In this way people feel they are really involved in the ownership of what goes on. They feel they really are participating in a collaborative partnership. Too many church meetings are dull, cosmetic consultations with speakers re-reading reports already circulated. No wonder they can be poorly attended, or full of in-fighting as people shout to make their voices heard.

Other kinds of mediation

There are many other kinds of mediation in which clergy and laity may become involved if they are asked to work as co-mediators in other agencies, or if they themselves act as volunteers there, as many Christians do.

Community mediation, especially for neighbours in conflict, is now available in most urban areas.

Environmental mediation specializes in dealing with noise and pollution conflicts, and is also a process used in large planning inquiries.

Evaluation mediation offers disputants who are blocked in their negotiations an expert assessment of the best way to resolve these. The decision remains theirs, so there is no arbitrated judgement.

Family mediation is now organized in statutory and voluntary services to help people separating and divorcing to co-operate over arrangements for their children and resources.

Medical mediation now has to be available for all NHS patients making complaints and seeking conciliation or compensation.

School mediation is used to train teachers and pupils in managing bullying and disputes, which include those involving parents.

Victim–offender mediation is used by probation services and their trained volunteers in rehabilitation and reparation work.

Commercial mediation is mainly known through the long-established work of ACAS, the Advisory, Conciliation and Arbitration Service. ACAS offers mediation. If parties cannot agree, ACAS can arbitrate, giving its own judgement, which is generally regarded as binding. There are also private commercial mediation and arbitration services which are useful for small businesses.

All of these services, and many others not mentioned here, rely on people with mediation skills, and it is to these that the next chapter turns.

> Put peace into each other's hands
> and like a treasure hold it,
> protect it like a candle-flame,
> with tenderness enfold it.
>
> *(Fred Kaan, 1929–)*

8 Practice in mediation

Peacemaking skills

I therefore, the prisoner in the Lord, beg you to lead a life worthy of the
calling to which you have been called, with all humility and gentleness, with
patience, bearing with one another in love, making every effort to maintain
the unity of the Spirit in the bond of peace.   *(Ephesians 4.1–3)*

Mothers, milkmen and miners make marvellous mediators! Conciliators need clear heads, kind hearts and common sense! These home-
made tongue-twisters point to peacemaking by ordinary people with
ordinary human abilities.

This chapter focuses on listing major peacemaking skills. It ends with
a short story of a mediation showing how some of these were used. It
begins by briefly considering ideas of personal qualities, abilities and
skills. In practice, many people use them interchangeably, but it can
be helpful to consider them separately.

Qualities of character are more concerned with our *being*, while abilities tend to describe our *doing*, and skills show good *practice*.

Paul wrote of the qualities of humility, gentleness and patience.
These are much needed in mediation, as are faith, hope and love, perseverance, honesty and humour, and many other good qualities. We
may have some of these, but most of us long to develop them over
our lifespan.

Using our abilities wisely can help this. The more we act sincerely
with people, the more will sincerity become established in our hearts.

Similarly, we can learn skills in improving our abilities, such as in
being able to talk with people without interrupting.

So our qualities, abilities and skills can become positively related in
helping us to develop our own personal potential, as well as that for
peacemaking. In fact many mediators experience the blessings of

valued personal growth over the years, whilst the most well-known among them are greatly respected for their characters.

However, as the opening sentences of this chapter suggested, peace-making is not just for the saints. The fact that we ourselves make mistakes and behave badly, should help us to understand how misunderstandings arise and what causes conflicts to occur.

Also, mediation is not just for the experts, although some are experts in it. We all have different temperaments and personal styles, which are useful to match in mediation. Naturally quiet people can be especially helpful to someone in conflict who is very shy. A more bubbly young mediator, using street-wise jargon, will obviously be able to strike a quick rapport with those having similar lifestyles.

So the list below has to be adapted to suit different personalities, and may be seen by some as qualities, some as abilities, and some as skills. It is stressed again that mediators need *training* and *practice* in these skills, generally by role play and exercises, especially in the company of other workers.

Above all, it is the *increasing practical experience* of mediating in real life situations from which we learn most. This is why it is so useful for individual Christians to work as volunteers in local mediation services, especially if these are developed by dioceses or ecumenical and other church circuits.

The list below can only be selective, and is alphabetical so as not to rank attributes artificially, as these are all of value. However, it is providential that active and attentive listening comes first in the list because this is surely a most important human skill. Indeed, we are made in the image of God, who is always actively and attentively listening to our prayers.

Active and attentive listening is what parents give to their children in serious trouble or illness, and what business people demonstrate when negotiating a deal. Mediators can show this by sincerity, stillness and silence, avoidance of negative interruptions and by positive body language (see below).

Affirm the value of people's positive agreement to mediate. Congratulate people on each stage of progress. Reinforce their productive efforts.

Arrange mediation room appropriately with comfortable chairs in circle. People in conflict face each other. Small tables can have flowers, water, tissues, paper and pencils for any note-taking (see below).

Attitudes of non-judgemental accepting people as they are with no personalized moralizing. Be compassionate, although firm if behaviour is unacceptable. This requires discernment (see below).

Avoid projection of own views and experiences about best ways of ending other people's conflicts. Respect their responsibilities for developing ideas. Give information rather than advice.

Awareness of mediators' own strengths and weaknesses, biases and values should be continuously developed.

Body language should be relaxed, encouraging rapport. Eye contact should be gentle and constant, but not staring. Caring facial expression should be responsive, but not over-reactive. Sit at friendly distances but not too close. Maintain upright posture with a slight forward listening inclination. Occasional, but not repetitive nodding and smiling encourages the hesitant. Make minimal movements of hands and limbs, avoiding crossing them tensely or twitching, and, unless co-mediator is present, touching people (see below).

Confidentiality and trust must be ensured by the warm way in which mediator(s) introduce the session and process, showing genuine concern for people. Continuing patient responses should be made to the ongoing questions they are invited to ask.

Compromise and concession can be aimed for, but not at the expense of personal rights to justice and fair dealing.

Control process not people by good ordering of mediation stages, firmly prevent interruptions or bad language, but avoid personal bossing and finger-wagging. Agree that a non-threatening raised hand calls for a minute's general silence.

Creative communication by clear, concise familiar words which show imaginative understanding of people's situations. Use open-ended and

'Who?', 'When?', 'What?' and 'How?' (rather than 'Why?') questions for fuller responses. Clarify confusions and misunderstandings. Be concrete in fact-finding. Enable people to focus on important points. Respect people's pauses. Encourage them in talking to each other, with eventual direct negotiation.

Decisions are not made by the mediators, but by the disputants. Their consent is sought to choices about timing and moving the mediation forward.

Discern need to intervene impartially and challenge offensive language or behaviour, explaining reasons for this. Warn that mediation will be stopped temporarily, if principles are breached. Allow time out to cool or refresh people. Discern need for coping with excess emotions (see below).

Emotional expression is encouraged so that people learn each other's feelings. Help them to distinguish facts from feelings. Enable them by empathy (see below) to control their excess emotions, crying, anger, etc. and congratulate their efforts. Offer water and tissues. When possible, avoid physical comforting in distress (hugging or holding hands). Mediators should provide good models of warm hearts but cool heads and contained emotion.

Empathy shows understanding of distress, while sympathy can suggest pity and personal identification with it. Avoid becoming emotionally involved with people's passions, or passivity.

Evaluation may be asked for, or offered, if there is a blockage. An impartial analysis can be given, and various suggestions made about different options for making progress.

Flexibility adapts the mediation process to special needs, and maintains healthy dynamics in discussions.

Humour helps to oil process but not at the expense of others.

Impartiality is shown by not taking sides between people, but does not mean being neutral about standing up for justice and power-balancing (see below).

Mini-meetings (or caucuses) inside the mediation may be needed. Mediator(s) can meet each person separately and confidentially by mutual request to discuss difficulties and ideas. These can only be relayed to the main meeting by permission. Mediators may also wish to meet on their own briefly to adjust their working together (see below).

Note-taking is sometimes vital in detailed discussion, but people should agree that records are temporary, anonymous and confidential.

Observing people's mannerisms carefully can give clues to their temperaments, but assumptions should not be made.

Openly identify discussion which discriminates against, stereotypes or victimizes people, and promote truth telling.

Perceptions are unique to each person. Help people to understand that events can be interpreted in different ways.

Power-balancing is needed if people have unequal resources, materially or mentally, etc. Mediators should explain that they will see that gifted talkers do not intimidate the shy. Disabled people may need their own advocates.

Problem-solving involves helping people to see their conflict in terms of difficulties of incidents and relationships which can be practically improved. Issues are listed and discussed.

Prospecting for options means helping people search for ideas for dealing with each issue, and listing these as above.

Reality agents are mediators who help people test each option to see if it will work in specific situations.

Reflect or feed back briefly but accurately what has been heard, preferably using matching words, checking for correctness.

Reframe discussion in positive terms if people speak destructively, whilst acknowledging difficulties.

Restructure and re-direct mediation process if people jump ahead to solutions before considering all options.

Role-exchange may help people see situations differently by 'putting on the other's shoes', or 'changing chairs'.

Summarize people's views as they develop, affirming each step of progress. When final agreements are reached, summarize these after checking accuracy, so that they can be written and signed.

Touching people can be misinterpreted, although co-mediation has safeguards. If acute distress leads to handholding, ask for people's consent.

Working together by mediators should model good co-operation in conversation and partnership in peacemaking. Generally (but not mechanically) take turns in talking. Show toleration but check any mistakes each makes. Provide support for one another, as well as for the disputants.

The case of the place in the church school

The Diocesan Mediation Service (DMS) had received an angry complaint from Cleo, saying that Fr Pat had discriminated against her racially and socially as a single parent. He had refused her child a place in the church school.

Fr Pat told the DMS that he wanted to save places for parish parents. He suspected that Cleo had just moved into the area to get better schooling.

After diocesan consultations about the suitability of mediation, the DMS co-ordinator invited Cleo and Fr Pat to accept this. They agreed. Two matched mediators were enlisted from a church in a different area. Grace was an Afro-Caribbean young mother, and Peter was a retired manager.

They welcomed Cleo and Fr Pat into a comfortable diocesan room, *arranged* so that the two women and two men sat next to one another in a circle.

They *affirmed* appreciation of the agreement to mediate. Peter explained briefly the principles and process of mediation, and the importance of listening to, and not interrupting each other.

Grace gave assurance about their *confidentiality, impartiality and non-*

judgemental attitudes, and said she hoped both would have *confidence and trust* in them, as mediators never made *decisions* for other people.

She turned towards Cleo (*affirmative body language*), and *attentively listened* to her account. Cleo said she and little Angie had moved because they had suffered racial persecution previously. She began to cry. Grace spoke comforting words, and the offered tissues were taken. After a pause, Cleo's *emotions were controlled*.

She said she belonged to a single parents' group. This had urged her to protest to the diocese when Fr Pat would not support giving Angie a place. It was thought that he was also a racist.

Fr Pat tried to interrupt with a denial, followed by an angry outburst from Cleo. Peter, *discerning* the need to *control the process*, held up his hand, and asked for a moment's silence. He asked them not to interrupt each other.

Grace then *reflected* back to Cleo the anger and distress she felt, and her need to find a good school for Angie.

Peter then asked Fr Pat for his side of things. He said he had many valued black members of his church. He did not know from Cleo's letter that she was an Afro-Caribbean. She had wrong *perceptions* about him. The reason he did not support her application was because he had to keep places for church parents.

Fr Pat would have talked at length about school affairs, but Peter was concerned to *power-balance* between the wordy minister and rather tongue-tied mother.

So Peter quickly thanked Fr Pat and gave a feedback of what had been heard. He checked that everyone agreed with the *summarizing*. He then asked them to list the *issues*.

Cleo said there were three. Discrimination against single parents. Racist attitudes to black school children. Arrangements for her Angie. Fr Pat said her unfair official complaint about him was the fourth.

Grace said they would deal with each issue in turn, and asked Cleo to say what she meant by, and how she had experienced, discrimination as a single parent (*creative communication*). Cleo said that she had married at 17 but her husband, a bike messenger, had been killed in a road accident. Grace showed *empathy*, saying that she understood the grief and loss, but *observed* that as Cleo wore no wedding ring, people didn't realize she was a young widow.

Grace then *openly identified* the general social problems of people either forgetting some single parents were widowed, or dividing them into harmful categories of the deserving and undeserving. Fr Pat admitted that his church took positive action by giving preference to widows. He said he was sorry he had wrongly assumed Cleo was not one.

Peter asked if this could lead to a *concession*, and Fr Pat agreed. But he refused to agree on the next issue of racism. He gave Cleo facts about the high number of black children in his school. So she admitted she had made a mistake about this.

Peter then suggested *flexibility* about going straight on to the fourth issue next. Cleo said she would not have made an official complaint had she known the truth about Fr Pat and was sorry about this.

Grace turned to the third issue about Angie's schooling and asked everyone to think of any options for *solving problems* about this. Fr Pat asked Cleo to become a church parent. She replied that she was not going to be bribed into religion. She asked how he would feel if he *changed roles* with her.

Grace, acting as a *reality agent*, said that pressure would be wrong and harmful, but asked how Angie would feel if all her school friends went to church, and she was left out.

Fr Pat then asked if Cleo would attend his school's parent education group, and allow Angie to come to Sunday children's service – if she wished. Cleo agreed.

Peter then congratulated them both on the progress they had made and suggested *testing the negotiations*. Would Fr Pat now be able to give a place to Angie? He said she could have the next vacant place, due the following month, but would want Cleo to withdraw her complaint from the diocese. Cleo agreed.

Grace and Peter said they both felt there was a basis for a written agreement about what offers had been made and *worked together* with the couple to list these as follows:

1 Cleo apologizes to Fr Pat and withdraws official complaints about him.

2 Fr Pat apologizes to Cleo for not recognizing her as a widow and arranges for Angie to have the next school vacancy.

3 Cleo will attend the parent education group and encourage Angie to go to Sunday church.

4 Fr Pat will always welcome Cleo or any single parent to his church.

Copies were made for Cleo, Fr Pat and the DMS confidential file. They were signed by the couple and the mediators. They thanked everyone for their co-operation. They would always be ready to re-convene the mediation, if future difficulties occurred. However, they felt sure that the couple would be able to sort these out themselves.

They reminded people that the statements were not legal documents, and suggested that they should all shake hands on the voluntary agreement.

This story may appear over-simplified. Yet it is a typical tale of an ordinary human conflict which could have had tragic social and church consequences if the press had magnified the misunderstandings and distorted the issues. It could have widened the trouble to include all the children, parents and teachers at the school, as well as all the parishioners, not to mention the bishop and diocesan staff.

The fact that the diocese had its own Diocesan Mediation Service was a crucial factor. It is by providing such services in diocesan areas, church circuits or through ecumenical co-operation, that inappropriate recourse to the formal and official sources of conflict management can be minimized.

Part Three considers these.

Kum ba yah, Lord,
kum ba yah,
someone's crying, Lord,
kum ba yah!
Someone's crying, Lord,
kum ba yah!
O Lord, kum ba yah.

(Traditional)

Peacemaking for Christians and churches:
Ways forward

The way of peace they do not know, and there is no justice in their paths.
Their roads they have made crooked; no one who walks in them knows
peace. Therefore justice is far from us, ... we wait for light, and lo! there is
darkness; ... We wait for justice, but there is none; ... Justice is turned
back, and righteousness stands at a distance;   *(Isaiah 59.8–9, 11, 14)*

He stood up to read, and the scroll of the prophet Isaiah was given to him.
... 'The Spirit of the Lord is upon me, because he has anointed me to bring
good news to the poor. He has sent me to proclaim release to the captives
and recovery of sight to the blind, to let the oppressed go free, to proclaim
the year of the Lord's favour.'   *(Luke 4.16–19)*

Do not judge, so that you may not be judged ... the measure you give will
be the measure you get.... You hypocrite, first take the log out of your own
eye, and then you will see clearly to take the speck out of your neighbour's
eye.   *(Matthew 7.1, 2, 5)*

9 Conciliation and the common good

Peacemaking for Christian communities

Whatever house you enter, first say, 'Peace to this house!' And if anyone who is there shares in peace, your peace will rest on that person, but if not, it will return to you.

(Luke 10.5–6)

This chapter briefly reviews the book's biblical grounding and its special focus on Jesus our mediator. It reconsiders the current context in which Christians and churches confront conflicts. It concludes by suggesting ideas for discussion with respect to future practical and positive action in peacemaking by Christian communities.

Jesus our mediator

Throughout the Old Testament we are given a picture of God as the one who is always ready to listen and reason with us about life's conflicts and crises. 'Come now, let us argue it out, says the LORD' (Isaiah 1.18).

The New Testament stories of Jesus also show him as the ready listener, who also commends listening to others: 'let anyone with ears to hear listen!' (Mark 4.9).

Yet Jesus knew how difficult it was for the disciples to listen with the open, attentive skills which this book has suggested we also may need to learn and practise. Even after the feeding of the five thousand, and the stilling of the storm on the lake, Jesus had to tell them that they had closed minds, and that 'their hearts were hardened' (Mark 6.52).

His ministry of love depended on people's hearts and minds being open, receptive and non-judgemental, so that they could experience God's peace in their own lives and be peacemakers with others. The First Epistle of John puts this more strongly:

Those who say, 'I love God,' and hate their brothers or sister, are liars; for those who do not love a brother or sister whom they have seen, cannot love God whom they have not seen.

(1 John 4.20)

Although this book has not focused on the deeper aspects of Christian love, or Christ's love, nor, as was stressed at its beginning, on all the many other divine and human roles and gifts which Jesus made manifest, some specially relate to his ministry of peacemaking.

The prophetic role of peacemaking

It is significant that Jesus defined his mission to the world in terms of Isaiah's famous recurring prophecies (42.1–7; 61.1, 8), about bringing healing to the broken hearted and justice to the nations. Luke (4.16–19), in the passage quoted earlier, shows the concern of Jesus for the poor, the captives, the blind and the oppressed.

In *Health is for God*, the former director of the Marylebone Healing Centre writes that

> The healing of relationships with other people is not merely a pastoral concern. It is also a prophetic one. It is about changing other people. It is about altering the environment. *(Hamel-Cooke, 1986)*

The fact that Jesus was crucified because his mission was thought to be a threat to the power of the politicians and religientsia, shows that his peacemaking was in the context of the real world. Yet his ministry as a mediator, like that of mediation, was not imposed, but offered. He was 'gentle and humble in heart' (Matthew 11.29), as mediators are required to be.

This prophetic role of peacemaking relates to the modern mediation context when conflicts involve Christians and churches. It can heal relationships. It is concerned to free people trapped in troubles. It offers awareness and clearer vision to those who have been blinded by mistakes and misunderstandings. It promises to preserve human rights by peaceful processes which promote co-operative and not oppressive behaviour. It tries to redress injustice by agreed reparation.

There is increasing concern to develop mediation values of consultation and collaboration, rather than competition, between social groups, and between government and citizens. In Britain, government stress on charters for social standards has developed a complaints culture. Increasingly people make complaints, rather than suffer in silence, or cripple themselves with the heavy costs of legal action, which is often inappropriate.

Suffering in silence has been a traditional halo for Christians. Yet for those who try to walk in the light, painful periods of darkness can become unbearable. This is especially so for those who have not learned to recognize the darkness within themselves, and thus magnify it in others.

As more and more people privately press or openly protest about contentious issues in society or church, bitter conflicts can develop. As we have seen, mediation skills can help people resolve these, as well as empowering them in personal and spiritual growth.

Here there is another link between mediation and the modern emphasis on encouraging personal and community decision-making at grassroots levels. Doctors typify this trend, when they increasingly ask us to participate in making decisions about what kind of treatment or care we want, especially in the closing stages of life.

There is also the related catholic notion of subsidiarity, recently adopted by the European Union. This is about decisions, especially social, economic and political ones, being made at the lowest effective level, rather than centrally. This adds to the current impetus for involving us, our churches and communities in the dialogues and discussions which often lead to conflict.

Here, the book's beginning is echoed in this concluding chapter. Mediation is the perfect process for this present time because it respects the positive aspects of conflict, and the rich diversity of human views. Yet it provides ways of comparing and making decisions about furthering these by acceptable human behaviour, not destructive conflict.

Mediation is also modest in its admission of failures, often in situations of personal and social sinfulness, as recognized by the writer to the Hebrews (Hebrews 6.4–6). Longdwelling hatreds and fears need deep healing before mediation can do its work. Mutual confession and forgiveness are needed.

Here it is interesting to note how often mediation and *meditation* are confused, when they can be so fruitfully combined. Many mediators practise meditation before and during intervals between ongoing cases. This is partly to enable them to develop interior spiritual peace and emotional management of work stress.

Meditation can also be offered to benefit those involved in the conflict, to help them manage their stress, anger and other emotions. If this becomes uncontrollably heated in a mediation session, a period of silence and reflection is often suggested, so that all concerned can become re-grounded in cooler calm.

Nor are blueprints promised in peacemaking. Although mediation processes have common patterns and skills, each session stresses that it is the people who are the parties to the conflict who determine progress and agreements.

Mediators, like the crucified Jesus, do not use their personal power to force people in any way. This leads to one aspect of peacemaking which is felt by some Christians to relate centrally to the prophetic role of Christ's ministry.

Peace movements organized by peace people, who are often involved in peace churches, have played an important historic part in awareness-raising and positive actions which spring from their belief in Jesus the peacemaker. Many have seen Christ's acceptance of the cross as the divine example of non-violent resistance to evil which they choose to follow in various ways, often in non-coercive mediation.

Although this book has avoided naming different denominations, it is fair to identify here the Quakers and Mennonites. They are respected for conscientious war relief work, while refusing to support the arms trade. Many of their values are based on Isaiah's related prophecies. 'The wolf shall live with the lamb ...' (Isaiah 11.6–9), and 'nation shall not lift up sword against nation' (Isaiah 2.4), were visions also supported by other prophets (Micah 4.3 and Joel 3.10).

These visions, and good works relating to them, led to Quakers and Mennonites being foremost amongst pioneers of the modern mediation movement.

They saw this as being a work of the Holy Spirit leading people to peacemaking in their personal and social conflicts, as well as in the wider tasks of international diplomacy and war prevention. Many of them have been among the first to volunteer to work in the present United Nations peacekeeping units around the world.

However, now Christians from the mainstream churches, and members of other religions or of none, are the increasing majority in the modern mediation movement.

They reflect the general public mixture of conservative as well as radical social views. Their political or cultural associations are never ethically allowed to influence their mediation work. If there is any possibility that anyone might consider there to be a conflict of ideas, loyalties or interests, other acceptable mediators are found.

So mediation in the modern context is a socially progressive movement in peacemaking, but carries no divisive labels. However, there are those who are suspicious that modern peacemaking means compromising justice, even though the prophets, old and new, have always proclaimed them to be twin aspects of the gospel. So the following brief section considers this.

Peace and justice

It is significant that an increasingly important and popular development has been the Roman Catholic organization, Pax Christi, which works for 'peace and justice'. It unites the religious, clergy and laity who are concerned that righteousness should be a governing principle in peacefully ordering church, national and international affairs, so that justice is done.

Pax Christi has special concern for the developing countries where the poor are subject to oppressive regimes, but its members only work for positive change in peacemaking ways. Mediation is seen as one of these. The international Roman Catholic St Egidio lay community also specializes in negotiated peacemaking.

Having said this, it is generally acknowledged that peacemakers have to work very hard to see that the process of mediation is not manipulated into persuading people to make agreements that perpetuate injustice and compromise their rights.

Similarly it is recognized that there are no simple answers to the great philosophical and practical problems about means and ends, lesser and greater evils, short and long-term benefits and absolute or relative values in negotiating agreements.

Mediation cannot be a panacea for peacemaking. There are too many structural injustices such as oppressive political regimes, economic practices and social discrimination, which have to be changed constructively in positive, practical ways that we have yet to devise.

It is sometimes even more difficult to distinguish between the law and mediation as the best first option in promoting justice. At early stages of most conflicts involving Christians and churches, mediation is often the most appropriate, and generally only approach needed.

Sometimes discussions reveal that illegal or criminal practices have taken place, and then mediators evaluate the ethical necessity for them to recommend that legal advice or action should be sought instead. Depending on the decisions people make, mediation can be suspended until the outcome of the alternative actions. This is because mediation may still provide a healing reconciliation if relationships resume, especially if court cases have humiliated people publicly. Mediation should never humiliate people, although it can help them to be humble.

However, there can be crises when sudden or continuing illegal, criminal or violent offences become revealed, where immediate recourse to the law, and possibly the police, is the obvious option. Even then mediation, with the consent of lawyers, or used by them, may play a final healing role in reaching agreements about forgiveness and reparation for wrongs done.

Whatever the situation, peace and justice have to be held in balance as central values. Here no stories are given as examples, as each situation is unique and has to be evaluated accordingly. Also human perceptions of peace and justice continually change.

This is where the flexible, here-and-now practical focus of mediation can offer more immediate readjustments to realities of present crises, or when developing injustices need remedies.

Mediation need never be a final process. Like ordinary daily bargaining between people, it can be resumed whenever new or changed solutions to conflicts need to be found. It is a dynamic process which serves our dynamic experience of daily life.

The final section of this concluding chapter suggests ways ahead for Christians and churches to consider providing practical opportunities for developing some of the mediation principles, processes and good practices outlined in this book.

Developing Christian and church mediation services

There are immediate opportunities in the UK for Christians, clergy and laity, to join their nearest community mediation service. Addresses are generally found in public libraries or town halls, or from the national voluntary organization Mediation UK, to which most belong, listed at the end of this book, as are other resources mentioned.

There they will receive good free training as voluntary mediators in return for undertakings to give agreed hours of service each month to the centre. They will then also be able to use their increasing skills in their own churches when occasions arise. Alternatively, they will be able to suggest that church friends should go to the community mediation service for more independent help.

Many Christians have chosen this path. Some of them have become leading officers of Mediation UK. Others have founded, chaired or directed a local community mediation service. Another group, the London Mennonites, have formed a bridge-building service specifically to help all denominational churches with conflicts. They also run training courses in mediating church conflicts which anyone can attend.

Other Christians have felt the call to work in the more intimately sensitive and specific areas of marriage mediation. This means applying to one of the local conciliation services, which in England and Wales are associated with the national voluntary organization, National Family Mediation.

Here they will face the more demanding, intensive and ongoing training that is required. They may have to agree to give more commitment and time to the work. In return, honorariums or higher expenses may be received.

This route may be useful to clergy who have a special interest in couples and families, just as marriage counselling training has also helped them in their pastoral care.

Clergy and laity who have close connections with hospital chaplaincy work and other health services, may wish to consider training as a lay conciliator in complaints procedures. These are now required by law, and are being developed in all health areas.

The National Health Service gives specialized and intensive training, and expects its conciliators to work on a set number of cases each year for which they receive a small fee.

There are further opportunities in the commercial and other fields mentioned earlier in this book, for people to learn and practise mediation. Particularly noteworthy is the concern of the London-based Centre for Dispute Resolution to develop a national initiative for managing church conflicts, and encouraging comprehensive discussion about this through networking with any interested forthcoming projects.

One important project is that being developed at St Ethelreda's church in London to serve as a centre for healing, peace and reconciliation, and as a sanctuary for victims and others in need of help.

Church conciliation or mediation services could be based on diocesan, regional, area or circuit boundaries, and each planned to reflect the interests and needs of different denominations. These could be linked with church pastoral care and disciplinary committees. They could thus provide conciliatory space and process in pastoral breakdowns before, or instead of, their submission to church tribunals or courts.

Churches working together for the common good

Another suggestion would be for mediation services to be ecumenically developed where local councils of churches found this to be most helpful. This would also provide an excellent example of co-operative relationships, and a wonderful witness to Christians peacemaking among themselves.

Unfortunately one of the constant criticisms of Christians as peacemakers is that the churches cannot agree among themselves. Shared mediation services would show that churches were responsibly trying to promote unity in diversity.

Whatever form mediation services took, they could have links, slight or strong, with relevant church regulatory and disciplinary frameworks mentioned in the previous chapter. They could also have links with church counselling services where these exist. In this way there could be early screening of which approach was most appropriate in the cases arising.

It is significant that the leading Christian writer, Susan Howatch, in her novel, *A Question of Integrity*, describes how the rector running a Healing Centre wants a fellow priest to act as a mediator between two clergy involved in a counselling conflict. Instead, a suicide resulted.

So it could also be suggested that healing centres should have staff trained in conciliation as well as counselling skills, and that their outreach publicity could mention the availability of mediation as an alternative or complementary form of healing and reconciliation.

In many cases, all these varied mediation services would merely enlarge existing good practice where informal conciliation is advised or offered before formal measures take place. The advantage would be that mediation was more openly known to be a service of the church.

This would encourage people to confront conflict earlier, because they would be assured that a confidential conciliation service was available. It would help to normalize the situations in which people can find themselves too often feeling guilty or afraid to approach their ministers.

The even greater advantage is the potential for personal and spiritual growth which mediation offers to all who take part in it.

We need to review how we act, and are perceived to act, with our co-members of the Body of Christ, or of our communities. We need to reconsider how our Christian faith is affecting the way we live, or would like to live in the future.

Paul gave similar encouragement to the early Christians and churches:

> We must no longer be children, tossed to and fro and blown about by
> every wind of doctrine, by people's trickery, by their craftiness in

deceitful scheming. But speaking the truth in love, we must grow up in every way...   *(Ephesians 4.14–15)*

Mediation, its principles, processes and services, have long traditions, but we need to develop them to fit the contemporary needs of churches working together for the common good.

These traditions stretch back to what has been called the 'palm tree justice' of early tribal societies, whose respected members dealt with disputes, and tried to reconcile people to face together the more crucial community tasks of survival in environments full of risks.

Interestingly, a member of a church in a developing country once commented that it was good that their valued and time-tested traditions of mediation were now being followed by Western Christians.

Western philosophers are also warning us that wars can be caused by global misunderstanding and miscommunication. They say that peacemaking through constructive communication is a corporate achievement of the highest moral and social order. People need to learn to talk together creatively at the highest as well as at grassroots levels.

Leading thinkers are also telling us that we live in 'a risk society' full of what they call 'managed uncertainties' and conflicts in every social area. The more risks and conflicts we have to negotiate in making personal choices and decisions, the more out of control we can feel. This is another reason for the churches to provide a supportive network of conflict management services.

In this respect, churches are often called 'mediating structures' because they serve protectively and positively between individuals and the dominating State and other authorities. If people deal early with their conflicts and problems through the services of their church, there may never be any need to become subject to the intervention or interferences of government and other agencies.

This recalls the story of the Israelites asking Samuel to give them kings to rule over them. God told Samuel to grant the request, as a second best, because the people no longer lived good lives respecting the rules of the Lord's law. So Samuel warned them that having governments like other nations would lead to their domination and oppression (1 Samuel 8.4–7; 10–22).

Today, of course, governments have become more democratic, and wisely know, like efficient business organizations, that the best way to make their members more co-operative, is to consult with them and enable them to be as self-determining as possible.

The principles of mediation have significantly contributed to these positive changes in practical as well as general ways.

British MBA courses for clergy now offer insights into conflict management, and these should include the biblical values of mediation described in this book. In this way, church administration will be based on Christian as well as business principles.

In the USA, the government uses a mediation process called 'negotiated rule-making' in which many of its administrative regulations are determined by detailed discussion by all those affected. They include representatives of citizen groups as well as relevant organizations. Of course, the basic laws are still made, as are ours, by parliamentary processes.

Another practical way in which mediation is being developed for the common good by progressive institutions lies in the increasingly important area of life-and-death decision-making.

Mediation processes are of great value in medical ethics, where patients, relatives, chaplains and other significant people's views need to be expressed and considered, as well as those of medical consultants and technologists.

Life-and-death decisions cannot just be left to the 'experts', particularly as these may change their minds as new knowledge and evidence is forthcoming. Even theologians have greatly varied views and conflicts of values.

Each individual person has unique needs, and mediation is a helpful process in protecting and promoting them. It also takes equal account of the needs of others who are affected by decisions, such as relatives and carers. In these sensitive areas, it can be provisional, and not definitive or final. It can gently lead people into searching for spiritual truth.

The Go-between God

This book has, from its beginning and biblical basis, tried to show how the spiritual truths which are the gifts of Jesus our mediator can be related to those on which human processes of mediation are developing.

Mediators are ordinary people who strive as go-betweens to enable people in conflict to make peace with each other. Christian peacemakers try to follow the leadings of the Holy Spirit, who Jesus promised would lead us into all truth. It was through the gradually unfolding teaching of the Holy Spirit that the early churches, actively working between Christians, were enabled and empowered to learn how to deal with their conflicts constructively.

However, they often failed, just as mediation fails, when human hearts are hardened and minds closed by the arrogance, self-centredness and sinfulness which needs humbling at the cross. This book has to conclude, as it began, by reminding ourselves that Christians cannot rely on peacemaking panaceas. We can only seek to learn from the wisdom of the word of God, and follow the example of Jesus the divine mediator, with the guidance of the Holy Spirit, as we seek to encourage our churches and the wider world in the paths of righteousness, justice and peace.

> Make me a channel of your peace,
>> where there is hatred,
>> let me bring your love.
> Where there is injury, your pardon, Lord,
>> and where there's doubt,
>> true faith in you.
>
>> *(St Francis of Assisi)*

Appendix: Consulting church codes

Discipleship and discipline

Now you are the body of Christ and individually members of it. And God has appointed in the church first apostles, second prophets, third teachers; then deeds of power, then gifts of healing, forms of assistance, forms of leadership...   *(1 Corinthians 12.27–28)*

As members of human groups, whether in our families, our churches or our country, we hope to find love, security and meaning in life. We try to be loyal to the values of our common bonds. We trust we will be protected from harm, and supported in our search for the common good.

Throughout human history, our churches have developed 'forms of assistance' and 'forms of leadership' to provide such guidance and support to those who want to become disciples of Christ. These have evolved variously into types of church government, including formal peacemaking processes.

The New Testament teaching of the apostles is firmly founded on the essential task of the early churches to provide structures of discipline and 'deeds of power' to enable its individual members to become bonded into the Body of Christ in the spirit of peace.

This appendix thus focuses on the importance of Christian disciples benefiting from and respecting the rules of their churches. Active members need to understand these, before challenging them, and contributing to their ongoing revision.

So this appendix points to the rules and regulations which some representative Christian bodies have developed to preserve order, doctrine and discipline, as they interpret this, and to protect the rights of members to worship and work together in peace.

However, members of individual Christian communities seeking to study their own church constitutions, any specific Standing Orders for membership and meetings, and other relevant rules and regulations, should apply to their headquarters for accurate detailed information, as only bare indications can be offered here of what is a changing administrative and legal landscape.

Addresses of major British churches can be found at the end of the book, to help readers further their inquiries.

Rules, regulations and rights

The early churches were based on the authority of Jesus himself (Matthew 28.18). Authority was extended to the disciples (Matthew 10.1; 18.18); to Peter in particular (Matthew 16.19); and also to all believers (John 1.12; 20.21).

This authority was mainly intepreted by the apostles in vertical or ranked levels of leadership which – to cut a long story short – eventually developed into major historic hierarchical forms of church government, in both Catholic and Protestant traditions, with clergy having main control. However, some Christians have also interpreted Jesus' warnings about ranked leaders, titles and power (Matthew 23.8–12) as showing his preference for what has been called delegated and democratic, or horizontal authority and leadership shared more fully with the laity. Though that is not to say that this strand of development has not produced hierarchies of its own.

Jesus, who saw himself not as a conquering king, but as the suffering servant of the Isaiah prophecies, and who washed his disciples' feet at the Last Supper, continually warned them about ranking themselves:

> But he said to them, 'The kings of the Gentiles lord it over them; and those in authority over them are called benefactors. But not so with you; rather the greatest among you must become like the youngest, and the leader like one who serves.'　　　　*(Luke 22.25–26)*

Thus different ideas of authority and leadership have contributed to the ways in which the churches have developed their forms of government and decision-making, depending on the social historic context.

We and the world have benefited by the enriching variety of Christian congregations which have resulted, and continue to emerge with ever-widening ranges of services on offer. However, we suffer endlessly from the confusions and conflicts which such differences cause, and from never-ending disputes about religious truths, or human beliefs about these.

This chapter does not enter into any ecumenical debate, or labelling, but tries to provide snapshots of the systems of authority on which mainstream churches base their rules and regulations, so as to understand the basis of their formal peacemaking in congregations.

These rules include governing the admission of members to churches, and can regulate their behaviour by expulsion, excommunication and disciplining, as well as by approval and reward. The ministry of clergy and church officers is generally subject to similar regulation.

Most modern systems of church government provide rights of appeal, although it is interesting that proposals for a Church of England's 1998 Churchwardens Measure gave bishops ultimate unappealable power to remove people from office who are judged to be continuing causes of conflict, when other means have failed.

Such Measures, and the rights of churches to regulate themselves, are generally upheld by state law, when clergy and congregational conflicts come before civil or criminal courts. For instance, a High Court or other judgement may reflect, or refer to, church law.

This church law is known as canon law in Roman Catholicism, Anglicanism and Orthodoxy, and has been laid down during past centuries. It is this, and the associated church courts, which we look at next, followed by considering some of the codes which other congregations follow for church discipline.

Canons, courts and codes

The 1983 revised code of Roman canon law continues to place the authority of the Pope as supreme, and located in the Vatican where the Congregation of the Doctrine of the Faith, the Congregation of Bishops and other appointed bodies, help him to control worldwide member churches, through encyclicals and other directives.

For the purpose of this book, comment is restricted to pointing out that the Pope even has power to make judgements in any local churches should he wish to intervene in serious conflicts, and to override the wishes of national conferences of bishops.

In practice, local church conflicts will generally first be considered by local parish councils and diocesan pastoral councils. However the Pope's appointed bishops regulate their dioceses, and contested cases are heard at their courts of first instance. These are diocesan tribunals in which the bishops are assisted by specialist clergy or laity trained in canon law.

Unresolved cases can go to the courts of second instance which are the provincial tribunals of archbishops, and are similarly tried according to canon law, always with rights of appeal.

Despite the fact that these courts are legalistic, and the canons are strictly formulated, many are tempered in practice by provisions which permit dispensations or exceptions. For instance, canon 1733 specifically advises conciliation in conflict. Others, such as 1676 and 1695, which apply to matrimonial matters, urge that all available pastoral means should first be used to heal individual, family and parish relationships.

There is thus space for priests and parishioners to develop mediation services. However, even such a welcome increase in democratic decision-making, consensus-building in conflict, and collaborative ministries would at present always be subject to the power of the Pope and priests in controlling church authority and discipline.

The Anglican Communion is also worldwide, but its authority is diffused, democratic and representative, based on synodical government. It is linked through the Anglican Consultative Council, and by Lambeth Conferences, which are held every ten years. Here archbishops, bishops, clergy and laity from different national churches discuss policies and develop church law.

The Anglican Communion is led by the Archbishop of Canterbury. He is counted as 'first among equals', and his formal power and control mainly consists in making influential recommendations in situations of conflict, whether worldwide, national or domestic, as well as promoting church law.

A member church, the Church of England, is state-established and subject to the monitoring of Parliament which, with the Sovereign as head of the Church, has to consent to any Measures of church law proposed by its General Synod. This is a representative body of elected clergy and laity, and the appointed bishops.

This church law has three integrated elements, which are compatible with each other, and with State law. There is historic canon law (which includes the constitution of courts), modified since the Reformation, and not codified as in Roman versions. There is church common law derived from accepted traditions, and church statute law such as framed in Measures passed by General Synod and ratified by Parliament.

Many of these Measures concern the powers and duties of Parochial Church Councils (PCC) which are elected bodies of the laity, with duties to consult and co-operate with the clergy, in promoting parish welfare and mission.

PCCs share responsibility with ministers for peacemaking in the parish, with old and new laws to help them, as a last resort. For instance an 1860 Ecclesiastical Courts Jurisdiction Act covers 'riotous, violent or indecent behaviour', while the 1993 Incumbents (Vacation of Benefices) [Amendment] Measure regulates serious pastoral parish breakdown.

These laws are administered in Church of England courts (often called Consistory, under the direction of judges called Chancellors) at diocesan and provincial levels with rights of appeal, which in some cases can extend to the Privy Council. The Court of Ecclesiastical Causes Reserved is only for clergy offences primarily related to doctrine and ritual.

Courts follow legal processes, with a bench of judges. Hearings are preceded by bishops' initial inquiries which, although judicially concerned to see whether there is a case to answer, also have conciliatory intent. If a case is proved, the bishop can censure, depose or disqualify ministers from service, as well as take other measures against ministers and laity recommended by the judges.

However, where possible, the Church of England avoids using its courts for dealing with the kind of congregational conflicts on which this book has focused. Persuasion and pressure are preferred in peacemaking. There are also opportunities for mediation skills and services to play a useful preventive role in dealing with church disputes.

The Methodist church is governed by the authority of its yearly elected Methodist Conference. Its constitution and Standing Orders have developed from its early organization based on presbyters or elders, although young people are now active as local lay church officers.

Conflicts and disciplinary matters involving ministers, deacons, lay preachers and church members can be dealt with in the courts of local churches, and in those of the wider district, circuit or connexional courts. Good standards of proof are required, and appeals can be made to the highest levels, and ultimately to the President of the Methodist Conference.

These courts are legally based and have strict rules based on judicial fairness. However, they are always preceded by conciliatory inquiries by church pastoral committees, who may find no case to answer. All hearings are before officers not involved in the complaint or conflict.

The Methodist Conference has been progressive in publishing central codes for dealing with cases of alleged sexual harassment and abuse, as have some other churches.

Methodists, through their Law and Polity Committee, also reviewed in 1996 the need to find a better balance for Christians between legal and pastoral procedures for dealing with disputes and disciplinary matters. There is renewed concern for congregational peacemaking, reconciliation and mutual forgiveness where possible. Thus here are opportunities for Methodists to benefit from absorbing more mediating skills and services into their churches.

The United Reformed Church, formed in 1972 by the union of a majority of Congregationalists and the Presbyterian Church of England, has, with the Church of Scotland, similar structures of authority, leadership, discipline, courts and codes as the Methodists, with the laity sharing power and control with ministers.

Baptist churches, however, have their authority located in their local church meetings, which independently develop their own constitutions, rules, regulations and discipline. Local congregations elect their own councils of deacons and elders, and choose their own ministers. They have teaching and training links with theological colleges and the Baptist Union, which gives their ministers formal recognition. Local churches are also associated in districts which have superintendents whose advice and intervention can be sought if congregational conflicts cannot be reconciled by the conciliatory means which are always pastorally preferred. There are no courts as such, but disciplinary hearings, if necessary, aim to be fair and impartial, observing judicial principles.

Here again the greater potential for locally shared power and control among church members and ministers, suggests that mediation skills and services could enrich their capacity for peacemaking.

Other disciples and disciplines

As well as the many other churches which have different degrees of authority, and varied patterns of leadership, two other well-known Christian bodies have distinctive ways of organizational peacemaking. The Salvation Army and the Religious Society of Friends (Quakers) are at extreme ends of the spectrum.

The Salvation Army has members who are soldiers and officers of Christ, subject to religious Articles of War, including rules and regulations about behaviour which are signed by recruits when they are sworn in and become members of corps with commanding officers and brigade leaders.

The Army has regular census boards which have a disciplinary function, but which give priority to advising, guiding, protecting and helping members 'under temptation' to bring about their 'restoration'. However, they can be suspended or removed from the rolls at quarterly or annual census meetings.

Despite the fact that the Army is organized on the hierarchical military model of command, it has a basic concern for peacemaking, rather like the State army's modern function of peacekeeping. It trains its officers in counselling and other communication skills. It could thus also enrich its work, especially with the vulnerable people it serves, by developing the ideas of Christian conflict resolution suggested in this book.

Quakers have been called Christians without creeds or clergy, whose authority is the Inner Light, which guided their founders over 300 years ago to develop a Covenant of Peace based on assemblies focusing on silent worship, charitable community service, and non-violence.

Quaker Faith and Practice is their book of Christian discipline, with coded requirements, recommendations and rebukes, rather than rules and regulations. This is revised periodically, but includes cumulative testimonies from the earliest years, to which any member can contribute.

Quakers are rightly respected as socially progressive people. An example of this is their ongoing practice of issuing recommendations giving guidance about dealing with disciplinary issues such as incidents involving discrimination or sexual offences.

There are clear processes for dealing with disputes, including 'clearness' and 'threshing' meetings, with rights to appeal. Mediation is mentioned in recent recommendations. There has also always been a traditional stress on settling conflicts by waiting on the Spirit, listening to each other, and discussing reconciliation. This has taken place in the open, practical context of local monthly meetings, small group and general meetings, and national yearly meetings.

Overseers and elders are elected by meetings, and although most officers work in a voluntary capacity, there are paid clerks and administrators responsible for meticulously kept records. Leadership roles are shared democratically on the basis of Friends being first among equals.

Although the Society is legally constituted, with the Meeting for

Suffering as an elected standing executive committee, it has no courts of its own, although its members, like those of the mainstream churches, owe obedience to the civil and criminal laws of the state.

Pentecostal and many other UK churches not so far mentioned are generally members of the Free Church Council and the Council of Churches for Britain and Ireland. They have their own constitutional identities, and systems of authority, regulation and discipline, and it is not within the scope of this appendix to give details of these. Information may be sought from the Councils, where addresses are given at the end of the book.

The Orthodox family of churches have their historic heartlands mainly in the East, with numerous congregations in the West. They have independent internal hierarchical administrations, with power and control exercised by patriarchs, bishops, priests and deacons. They acknowledge the overarching authority of the Ecumenical Patriarch of Constantinople.

Orthodox spirituality is a Christian treasure widely written about, but little is published in the West relating to their church management, rules and regulations. Their reliance on 'sobernost', the unity of many persons within the organic fellowship of the church, with each person having full freedom and personal integrity, suggests that conflicts are approached in conciliatory ways. It is interesting that the deeply respected Bishop Kallistos of Diokleia has pointed to the fact that Christians share Christ's vocation in mediation.

New directions in discipleship and discipline

These inadequate sketches cannot portray all the other varied developments which are continually taking place in the wider world, such as in the 'base communities' of Latin America, with their concern for peacemaking and justice. Thus it is hoped that this book will encourage as many Christian communities as possible, far and near, small and large, to share with us their valuable experiences in peacemaking.

Religious communities study, pray and promote peacemaking, with ideas for reforming church life. Similarly, the charismatic and house church movements have all contributed to ideas of authority as an evolving gift of the Holy Spirit in the renewal and reconciliation of Christians.

Christian radical, conservative and fundamentalist groups work in and between denominations to change informal and formal power structures. Some suggest that these, and State law, are only valid if they fulfil divine law. However this is always differently interpreted by humans, and God cannot appear in the dock.

We also have much to learn from Christians and churches suffering from oppression and persecution in the developing countries, and how they are struggling to build peace, while resisting domination by others.

All of this is evidence of the rich vitality and plurality of the Christian churches, their ministers and laity in seeking to build firmer foundations of justice to support the gospel of peace.

These established foundations of justice, based on the church law structures and systems at which this chapter has glanced, are also evidence of the great achievements of Christianity in setting forth standards of conduct and public accountability, which can be openly defined and contested. Its canons, courts and codes are part of Western civilisations' contribution to the democratic ordering of human society.

That does not, of course, mean that the debt is all one-way. Churches today, especially in their roles as employers or as partners with the state in providing education, may find their behaviour at odds with current legislation or best practice. But this is an argument for seeking to discuss the right way to revise church procedures, not to abolish them.

Churches may be mocked for behaving badly, and for needing courts to judge them, but Christian discipleship needs purifying and strengthening discipline, and clear directions about its duties, for the work of peacemaking to progress.

Thus church leaders, administrators, lawyers and mediators all share in the same valuable task of working together, although in different ways and at different times, for the common good. As Paul said, 'Let all things be done for building up' (1 Corinthians 14.26): building up communities of love based on justice and law, a Christian model for humanity, and the work of God.

What can we do to work God's work,
to prosper and increase
the brotherhood of all mankind,
the reign of the Prince of Peace?
What can we do to hasten the time,
the time that will surely be,
when the earth shall be filled with the glory of God,
as the waters cover the sea?

(A. C. Ainger, 1841–1919)

Prayers for peacemaking

Adapted and abridged with gratitude to past and present peacemakers,
for use in preparing for, beginning and closing mediation, and in pauses
for reflection

Almighty God
from whom all thoughts of truth and peace proceed;
kindle, we pray, in the hearts of all people
the true love of peace;
and guide with your pure and peaceable wisdom
those who take counsel for the nations of the earth;
that in tranquillity your kingdom may go forward,
till the earth is filled with the knowledge of your love;
through Jesus Christ our Lord.

———————

O God,
the source of all good desires,
all right judgements, and all just works:
give to your servants that peace
which the world cannot give;
that our hearts may be set to obey your commandments,
and that freed from the fear of our enemies,
we may pass our time in rest and quietness;
through Jesus Christ our Lord.

———————

Merciful God,
grant to your faithful people pardon and peace:
that we may be cleansed from all our sins

and serve you with a quiet mind;
through Jesus Christ our Lord.

————

O God,
when you give to your servants
to endeavour in any great matter,
grant us to know that it is not the beginning
but the continuing of the same
until it be thoroughly finished
which yields the true glory.

————

Almighty God, help us
to do all the good we can, by all the means we can,
in all the ways we can, in all the places we can,
at all the times we can, to all the people we can,
as long as we can.

————

Merciful God,
may everything we do
begin with your inspiration,
continue with your help,
and lead to peace with your guidance and love.

Lord,
to you there is no high, no low, no great, no small:
your love fills, binds, connects us all.

*   *   *   *

Lord,
what is rigid, gently bend,
what is frozen, warmly tend.

Lord,
help us to think clearly, speak gently,
love truly, act peaceably.

Lord,
your kingdom of peace is with us:
help us to open the door and enter in.

Lord,

prevent us from taking an eye for an eye,

lest we become blind.

Lord,

help us not to belittle others,

so as to increase ourselves.

Lord,

help us to be masters of ourselves,

that with you we may be servants of others.

Lord,

help us not to lose ground by throwing mud

which we need for building peace.

Lord,

help us not to judge others

until we have walked in their moccasins for many moons.

Lord,

let that which seems impossible by our nature,

become possible by your grace.

Lord,

help us focus on our own failings,

more than on the faults of others.

Lord,

help us to see ourselves and others as we truly are,

and shall be, when you have finished your work in us.

Lord,

there is no sin that you cannot forgive,

there is no sickness that you cannot heal.

Lord,

help us to do the good in the present and future

instead of grumbling about the past.

*　*　*　*

Holy Spirit,
grant us so to strive and act
that those things which cloud my own ways
may not darken the paths of others.

————

Holy Spirit,
help us to learn silence from the talkative,
toleration from the intolerant,
kindness from the unkind,
and justice from the unjust.

————

Holy Spirit,
you are the way to peace and justice:
by your power break the barriers which separate us,
melt our hearts that are hardened
and help us to bow to one another,
casting out fear with true repentance,
as you fill us with your perfect love.

————

Holy Spirit,
give us time for the task,
wisdom for the work,
inner peace and grace,
and faith in your power.

————

Holy Spirit,
help us to change that which can be altered,
explain that which can be understood,
teach that which can be learned,
revise that which can be improved,
resolve that which can be settled,
so that love, peace and justice may come together.

*   *   *   *

O Lord – Creator, Son and Holy Spirit,
you have taught us who minister in your church
to be the willing servants of others:

give us skill and gentleness
in the practice of our ministries,
and perseverance always in prayer.

————————

O Lord – Creator, Son and Holy Spirit,
support us all the day long of this troublous life,
until the shadows lengthen and the evening comes,
and the busy world is hushed,
and the fever of life is over, and our work is done:
then, Lord, in your mercy, grant us safe lodging,
a holy rest, and peace at the last.

————————

O Lord – Creator, Son and Holy Spirit
bless us and keep us,
make your face shine upon us
and be gracious to us,
look kindly on us,
and give us peace,
now and always.

Church contact addresses

Action of Churches Together in Scotland
Scottish Churches House, Kirk Street, Dunblane, Perthshire, F15 0AJ
T: 01786 823588
F: 01786 825844

Baptist Union of Great Britain
Baptist House, PO Box 44, 129 The Broadway, Didcot OX11 8RT
T: 01235 512077
F: 01235 811537

Catholic Bishops' Conference of England and Wales
39 Eccleston Square, London SW1V 1PD
T: 0171 630 8220
F: 0171 630 5166

Catholic Bishops' Conference of Ireland
Iona, 65 Newry Road, Dundalk, County Louth, Republic of Ireland
T: 00 353 42 38087
F: 00 353 42 33575

Catholic Bishops' Conference of Scotland
64 Aitken Street, Airdrie, Lanarkshire ML16 6LT, Scotland
T: 01236 764061
F: 01236 762489

Church in Wales
Cathedral Road, Cardiff CF1 9XF
T: 01222 231638
F: 01222 387835

Church of England General Synod
Church House, Great Smith Street, London SW1P 3NZ
T: 0171 222 9011
F: 0171 799 2714

Church of Ireland
Church of Ireland House, Church Avenue, Rathmines, Dublin 6, Irish
Republic
T: 00 353 1 4978422
F: 00 353 1 4978821

Church of Scotland
121 George Street, Edinburgh EH2 4YN
T: 0131 225 5722
F: 0131 220 3113

Churches Together in England
Inter-Church House, 35–41 Lower Marsh, London SE1 7RL
T: 0171 620 4444
F: 0171 928 5771

Churches Together in Wales
First Floor, 21 St Helen's Road, Swansea SA1 4AP
T: 01792 460876
F: 01792 469391

Council of African & Afro-Caribbean Churches
31 Norton House, Sidney Road, London SW9 0UJ
T: 0171 274 5589

Council of Churches for Britain & Ireland
Inter-Church House, 35–41 Lower Marsh, London SE1 7RL
T: 0171 620 4444
F: 0171 928 0010

Free Churches Council
27 Tavistock Square, London WC1H 9HH
T: 0171 387 8413
F: 0171 383 0150

Greek Orthodox Church
5 Craven Hill, London W2 3EN
T: 0171 723 4787
F: 0171 224 9301

Irish Council of Churches
Inter-Church Centre, 48 Elmwood Avenue, Belfast BT9 6AZ
T: 01232 663145
F: 01232 381737

Lutheran Council of Great Britain
30 Thanet Street, London WC1S 9QH
T: 0171 383 3081
F: 0171 383 3081

Methodist Church Conference Office
25 Marylebone Road, London NW1 5JR
T: 0171 486 5502
F: 0171 224 1510

Religious Society of Friends
Friends House, 173 Euston Road, London NW1 2BJ
T: 0171 663 1000
F: 0171 663 1001

Russian Orthodox Church Abroad
Church House, 57 Harvard Road, London W4 4ED
T: 0181 742 3493
F: 0181 995 9503

St Ethelreda's Church
14 Ely Place, London EC1 6RY
T: 0171 405 1061
F: 0171 405 7440

Salvation Army
101 Queen Victoria Street, London EC4P 4EP
T: 0171 332 0022
F: 0171 236 6272

United Reformed Church in the UK
86 Tavistock Place, London WC1H 9RT
T: 0171 916 2020
F: 0171 916 2021

Full details of all churches, Christian organizations and networks are in the annual *UK Christian Handbook*, see Further Reading.

Mediation contact addresses

Advisory, Conciliation and Arbitration Service (ACAS)
Head Office, Brandon House, 180 Borough High Street, London SE1
1LW
T: 0171 210 3613
F: 0171 210 3645

Centre for Dispute Resolution (CEDR)
Princes House, 95 Gresham Street, London EC2V 7NA
T: 0171 600 0500
F: 0171 600 0501

Family Mediation Cardiff
4th Floor, St David's House, Wood Road, Cardiff CF1 1EY
T: 01222 229692
F: 01222 399505

Family Mediation Scotland
127 Rose Street, South Lane, Edinburgh EH2 4BB
T: 0131 220 1610
F: 0131 220 6895

Family Mediation Service
Irish Life Centre, Lower Abbey Street, Dublin 1 Eire
T: 00 353 1 8728277
F: 00 353 1 8787497

Jewish Arbitration and Mediation Service (JAMS)
c/o Stuart Young House, 221 Golders Green Road, London NW11
9DQ
T: 0181 922 2000
F: 0181 922 1998

Mediation UK
Alexander House, Telephone Avenue, Bristol BS1 4BS
T: 0117 904 6661
F: 0117 904 3331
Details of community mediation services, publications lists, general training manual and trainers' directory on request.

Mennonite Bridge Building in Congregational Conflict
London Mennonite Centre, 14 Shepherds Hill, London N6 5AQ
T: 0181 340 8775
F: 0181 341 6807
Specialized training workshops, publications and mediation services for all denominations.

Multifaith and Multicultural Mediation Service
c/o 4 Woollas Hall, Bredon Hill, Nr Pershore, Worcs WR10 3DN
T: 01386 750965
F: 01386 750965

National Family Mediation
9 Tavistock Place, London WC1H 9SN
T: 0171 383 5993
F: 0171 383 5994
Lists of services, publications and training courses.

Relate Northern Ireland
76 Dublin Road, Belfast BT2 7HP
T: 01232 322914
F: 01232 315298

Further reading

Acland, A., *A Sudden Outburst of Common Sense*. Hutchinson Business Books, London, 1990.

Behrens, J., *Practical Church Management*. Gracewing, Leominster, 1998.

Brierley, P. and Wraight, H. (eds), *UK Christian Handbook 1996/1997*. Evangelical Alliance, London, 1998.

Burnside, J. and Baker, N., *Relational Justice*. Waterside Press, Winchester, 1993.

Coffey, D., *Build That Bridge*. Kingsway Publications, Eastbourne, 1986.

Cormack, D., *Peacing Together*. MARC Monarch Publications, Eastbourne, 1989.

Cornelius, H. and Faire, S., *Everyone Can Win*. Simon & Schuster, London, 1989.

Craig, Y. (ed.), *Advocacy, Counselling and Mediation in Casework*. Jessica Kingsley Publishers, London, 1998.

De Bono, E., *Conflicts*. Penguin, Harmondsworth, 1986.

Donohue, W. and Kolt, R., *Managing Interpersonal Conflict*. Sage, London, 1992.

Fisher, R. and Ury, W. *Getting to Yes*. Arrow, London, 1990.

Hamel-Cooke, C., *Health is for God*. Marylebone Health Centre, London 1986.

Howatch, S., *A Question of Integrity*. Little Brown, London, 1998.

Macmorran, K. and Briden, T., *A Handbook for Church Wardens and PCC Councillors*. Mowbray, London, 1997.

Moore, C., *The Mediation Process*. Jossey-Bass, San Francisco, 1986.

Peters, D., *Surviving Church Conflict*. Herald Press, Scottdale, PA, 1997.

Religious Society of Friends (RSF), *Quaker Faith and Practice*. RSF, London, 1994.

Roberts, M., *Mediation in Family Disputes*. Wildwood/Gower, London, 1988.

Spinks, T. and Clements, P., *A Practical Guide to Facilitation Skills*. Kogan Page, London, 1993.

Taylor, J., *The Go-Between God*. SCM Press, London, 1972.

Wright, M. and Galway, B., *Mediation and Criminal Justice*. Sage, London, 1989.

Index

The Society for Promoting Christian Knowledge (SPCK) was founded in 1698. It has as its purpose three main tasks:

- **Communicating the Christian faith in its rich diversity**
- **Helping people to understand the Christian faith and to develop their personal faith**
- **Equipping Christians for mission and ministry**

SPCK Worldwide serves the Church through Christian literature and communication projects in over 100 countries. Special schemes also provide books for those training for ministry in many parts of the developing world. SPCK Worldwide's ministry involves Churches of many traditions. This worldwide service depends upon the generosity of others and all gifts are spent wholly on ministry programmes, without deductions.

SPCK Bookshops support the life of the Christian community by making available a full range of Christian literature and other resources, and by providing support to bookstalls and book agents throughout the UK. SPCK Bookshops' mail order department meets the needs of overseas customers and those unable to have access to local bookshops.

SPCK Publishing produces Christian books and resources, covering a wide range of inspirational, pastoral, practical and academic subjects. Authors are drawn from many different Christian traditions, and publications aim to meet the needs of a wide variety of readers in the UK and throughout the world.

The Society does not necessarily endorse the individual views contained in its publications, but hopes they stimulate readers to think about and further develop their Christian faith.

For further information about the Society, please write to:
SPCK, Holy Trinity Church, Marylebone Road,
London NW1 4DU, United Kingdom.
Telephone: 0171 387 5282